WOMAN IN YORKIST ENGLAND

by

Darlene Tempelton
Catholic Central High School
Springfield, Ohio

Mesquite   1984

Ide House

Published by
Ide House, Inc.
4631 Harvey Drive
Mesquite, Texas 75150-1609

© 1983, Darlene Tempelton

Of the Ide House series **Woman in History** *this is*
volume 49

Library of Congress Cataloging in Publication Data

Tempelton, Darlene, 1953-
  Woman in Yorkist England.

  (Woman in history; ISSN 0195-9743 ; v. 49)
  Bibliography: p.
  Includes index.
  1. Women--England--Social conditions. 2. Women--
England--History. 3. Great Britain--History--Lancaster
and York, 1339-1485. I. Title. II. Series.
HQ1593.T45 1984   305.4'0942   83-22776
ISBN 0-86663-051-1
ISBN 0-86663-052-X (pbk.)

ISSN for the Ide House *Woman in History* series is ISSN 0195-9743 of which
this is volume 49.

This book is dedicated to the two men who have supported and encourage me in my study of history:

my father:
Donald C. Tempelton

my husband:
Daniel V. Kempf

Thank you.

TABLE OF CONTENTS

Historical Introduction 1

Chapter One 13
Education

Chapter Two 21
Marriage

Chapter Three 41
Daily Life
The Gentry
The Merchant/Middle Class
The Peasant

Chapter Four. 59
Women in the Wars of the Roses

Select Bibliography 82

Index. 85

About the Author 89

ENGLAND & IRELAND

Historical Introduction

Now is the winter of our discontent
Made glorious summer by this House of York.
                                    −Richard III
                                    Shakespeare

Indeed the Yorkist Age was a time of summer for the people of Merry Old England. A transitional period in British history, it bridged the gap between the Middle Ages and the Tudor Age. It contained much of the best and little of the worst of both epoch periods.

The Yorkist Age spanned a relatively brief period of time in history. Although there are no firm dates by which it can be delineated, at its earliest one can say that it began with the first battle of St. Albans in 1455, and ended in 1487 at the Battle of Stoke. This unique Age in the history of the English people is wonderfully woven in the threads of a rich tapestry of battle, intrigue and glory in high places, yet, the actions of the king and of his court rarely played directly or intimately in the daily script of life which affected the existence of the majority of the English people.

The first Yorkist king, Edward IV (1442-1483)[1] ascended the throne in 1460, after five years of intermittent warfare between his father Richard, Duke of York,[2] and the followers of King Henry VI.[3] Edward had a very tenuous claim to the throne he usurped from his cousin Henry. According to the laws of succession, upon Henry's death the crown should have gone to his son, Edward of Lancaster. But Henry's long reign[4] was unstable, with Henry himself prone to periods of insanity.

The actual job of ruling devolved upon Henry's wife, Queen Margaret of Anjou,[5] and his cousin Beaufort, Duke of Somerset.[6] Richard, Duke of York, felt that the Queen and her advisors excluded him from his rightful place in the governance of the realm. Not only was Richard, as Duke of York, a powerful peer, but he was also the king's cousin,[7] and, until Henry's son Edward was born in 1453, the heir-presumptive to the throne.[8] The *Croyland Chronicle* describes the situation in England during the period 1450-1460:[9]

> . . . you might plainly perceive public and intestine broils fermenting among the nobles of the realm. . .; one party adhering to the king, while the other, being attached to the duke [of York] by blood or by ties of duty, sided with him. The consequence was that . . . the combatants on both sides, uniting their respective forces together, attacked each other whenever they happened to meet, and, quite in accordance with the doubtful issue of warfare, now the one and now the other, for the moment gained the victory . . . . In the meantime, however, the slaughter of men was immense; for besides the dukes, earls, barons, and distinguished wariors who were cruelly slain, multitudes almost innumerable of the common people died of their wounds. Such was the state of the kingdom for nearly ten years.

As can be seen in the above quote, years of verbal assaults led to the clash of metal against metal on the battlefield.

The first battle, that of St. Albans in 1455, was followed by five years of intermittent warfare between the armies of the Queen and the Duke. This only ended with the death in battle of Richard of York at Wakefield in 1460, and the subsequent offer by Parliament of the crown to York's eldest son, Edward. Queen Margaret attempted to regain the throne, but all her attempts ended in failure and she was finally forced to flee the country with her young son. King Henry, her husband, was honorably imprisoned within the Tower of London.

The people of London were greatly impressed with their new king. Edward began immediately healing the wounds caused by years of civil war between his father and the exiled Queen by pardoning such ardent Lancastrians as Beaufort, Duke of Somerset,[10] and John de Vere, Earl of Oxford.[11]   Perhaps his choice of Elizabeth Woodville,[12] as his wife was part of his attempt at reconciliation, for she was the widow of a Lancastrian knight who died fighting for Margaret at St. Albans. This marriage may have pleased the common people, but unfortunately it alienated many members of the nobility and the royal family who had looked to a foreign marriage alliance, and who also disliked seeing someone of lesser standing than they, lifted above them.

In 1469, Edward's cousin, Richard, Earl of Warwick,[13] unexpectedly allied himself with the exiled Queen Margaret, and led a revolt against the King, tearing apart the fine fragile fabric of peace that Edward had woven across the country. Because the two had been close friends, Warwick's rebellion was difficult for Edward to accept—but it was not totally unexpected. Warwick was one of the wealthiest and most powerful men in England. He had used both his wealth and his power to help his cousin obtain the throne. He had probably hoped to be the king's foremost advisor, but Edward was strictly an   individual—in every sense; he refused to let anyone make decisions for him.

The area in which the two men most strongly disagreed was in the arena of foreign affairs. Edward wanted an alliance with the Duchy of Burgundy, and was negotiating with Duke Philip to marry his sister Margaret to Philip's son Charles. Warwick perferred a French alliance, and had been negotiating with the French king, Louis XI, to marry Edward to the king's sister-in-law, Bona of Savoy, when the continent vibrated with the unexpected and startling news arrived that Edward had already married Elizabeth Woodville.

Warwick strongly disapproved of Elizabeth. He felt that Edward's new wife was totally unqualified to be England's queen. He also disapproved of her family—and the increasing influence which they had over the king.

In 1467, Warwick began to contemplate treason against his leige-lord and friend. He clandestinely convinced Edward's eighteen-year-old brother, George, Duke of Clarence,[14] to join him. Then, in June, 1468, some of Warwick's retainers incited several small rebellions in Yorkshire. In July, Warwick publically set forth his grievances against the King. Earnestly exclaiming against Edward's exclusion of Edward's "blood relatives" from his secret council while depending upon the Woodvilles for advise in the governance of the English realm, Warwick denounced the developments in no uncertain language. On July 29, 1468, Warwick set out for the highest prize, and captured the King himself. A few days later he seized and executed the Queen's father, Lord Rivers, and her younger brother, John.

Warwick found that in capturing the King he had not obtained the power and prestige he sought. Edward's supporters refused to co-operate with the wiley Warwick, and without their assistance and allegiance, Warwick discovered that he was powerless to govern. In October, Edward was freed and allowed to return to his capital city, London.

Although the King was set free, Warwick's rebellion was not over. In 1470, Warwick rose again against the King; again Warwick was defeated.

In the ignomy of defeat Warwick fled to France. Once across the Channel, Warwick enlisted the aid of the ever conspiring French sovereign, Louis XI.[15] Closeted with the French King, Warwick laid out his plans to cross back over the Channel, and returning to England, raise an army, defeat Edward, and exiling (or killing?) the King, returned the old king, Henry VI, to the English throne. Louis accepted Warwick's proposals.

Warwick embarked for England with French troops supplied by the French king on September 9, 1470. Swiftly they crossed the Channel.

Landing on English soil, Warwick and his conscripted calvary and foot-soldiers, found new support among the old Lancastrian nobles- and among others, who, for various reasons, were increasingly discontented with Edward's governance of the English realm. Suddenly Edward found himself surrounded by hostile troops. (Barely the young King escaped with his life.)

Seeking foreign sanctuary, Edward found refuge with his brother-in-law, the Duke of Burgundy. Detailing his plight, Edward was able to borrow from Philip both troops and money. Supplied with what he needed to wrestle with Warwick for the right to sit upon the English throne, Edward returned to England in March, 1471.

On Easter Sunday, April 14, Edward's army clashed with Warwick's at Barnet. A four hour battle ensued; both troops were blinded by a thick fog which settled over the area, causing some of Warwick's men to mistake their own coterie for the enemy, slaying many who heralded Warwick's colors. During the route that followed Warwick, himself, was slain.

Later that day, Queen Margaret of Anjou landed on English soil with her personal army. Hearing of the disasterous defeat of her recent ally, the Earl of Warwick, she turned and prepared to cross back to France. She was stopped, however, being convinced by her supporters that there was still a chance for victory. Pledging to remain in England, Margaret of Anjou, determined to fight for the throne that eluded her grasp.

On May 4, Margaret's tired troops treked toward's Edward's encampment at Tewkesbury. A battle ensued.

During the carnage which followed, Margaret's son was killed. The next day Margaret, herself, was captured.

On May 21, King Henry VI, died in his chambers in the Tower. The official record relates that his death was due to "pure displeasure and melancholy,"[16] at learning of the death of his son and the capture of his wife. However, it was common knowledge, as the Milanese ambassador to France reported, that "King Edward caused King Henry to be secretly assassinated".[17] Edward was now indisputably King of England.

For the next twelve years, Edward ruled a country at peace with increasing prosperity. He continued his policy of conciliation with Lancastrian rebels, allowing their sons and heirs to inherit their father's titles, and, at least a portion, of their lands. He, furthermore, encouraged trade with foreign countries, going so far as to lower tariffs, so that new commodities could be brought into the England. At the same time Edward protected the goods which were manufactured in England from unfair foreign competition.[18] His trade agreements and concessions were full-bodied, determined, and detailed:[19]

> This same king in person, having equiped ships of burden, laded [sic] with the finest wools, cloths, tin, and other products of his realm, and, like a man living by merchandize, exchanged goods for goods, both with the Italians and the Greeks, through his factors.

Edward proved so successful in his financial dealings that he paid off the considerable debts that had accumulated during the reign of Henry VI. For the first time in many years the crown lived off its own income without raising taxes. Because of this, the middle class—the bourgoise businessmen—loved Edward.

At the same time as he promoted international commerce, Edward insured the peace. Signing a treaty of peace with France which assured the English King that the French sovereign would no longer conspire against his rule by plotting with usupers or pretenders to the English throne, Edward ended English aspirations to the French throne, and thus wrested a promise of no future threats of foreign invasion from the French coast by Frenchmen.[20] To insure internal peace, Edward instituted in England two councils along the Welsh and Scot borders. The Council of the North, led by Edward's brother Richard, kept order in Yorkshire and along the border of Scotland. The other council, based at Ludlow, directed by the Queen's brother, Anthony, Lord Rivers, kept order in Wales.

In spite of these successes and promises of prosperity and continued peace both at home and abroad, the dissatisfaction felt by many members of the nobility could not be hidden.[21] The Queen and her family were hated covertly and overtly by the King's own relatives. Dissension even arose between and among the members of Edward's immediate family. George, Duke of Clarence, Edward's younger brother, constantly involved himself in pursuits that bordered on being treasonous. He had been involved in Warwick's rebellions in 1468, and in 1470. In 1471, George had tried to block the marriage of his youngest brother, Richard,[22] to Warwick's daughter, Anne.[23] George was married to Anne's sister, and he did not wish to share the immense Warwick inheritance with anyone. Finally, in 1477, George arrested, tried and executed a gentlewoman, Ankarette Twynho, whom he accused of having poisoned his wife and infant son.[24] Soon after this incident, Edward had George arrested and prosecuted for treason. On February 18, 1478, the Duke of Clarence was privately executed in the Tower, possibly, as legend has it, by drowning in a butt of malmsey wine.[25]

Edward's youngest brother, Richard, Duke of Gloucester, remained loyal to the King but preferred to remain on his Yorkshire estates away from the royal court.

Rumor has it that Richard and the Queen disliked one another intensely. Richard certainly blamed Elizabeth and her family for Clarence's death.[26]

On April 9, 1483, Edward suddenly died after a short illness. He left his twelve year old son, Edward V (1470-1483),[27] as heir to the throne. Edward's will established a Council of Regency, composed of members of the Queen's family and Edward's closest friends to guide the youth. The council was to be led by Richard, Duke of Gloucester, who was given the title of Lord Protector. Queen Elizabeth, perhaps out of distrust for Richard, or perhaps in an attempt to gain power for herself, attempted to prevent Richard of Gloucester from taking his seat on the Council by neglecting to inform him of Edward's death. She apparently hoped to have her son safely in London and in her care before Richard could leave his Yorkshire home. But, another council member, aware of the plot, wrote to Richard, advising him:[28]

> The King has left all to your protection—goods, heir, realm. Secure the person of our sovereign Lord Edward V and get you to London.

Richard did, and took custody of the young king at Northampton, about a day's march north of London. At the same time he arrested the young Edward's guardian, Anthony, Earl Rivers, and his half-brother, Richard Grey. Queen Elizabeth, upon hearing this, fled into Westminster Sanctuary with her daughters and her younger son, Richard, Duke of York.

The dead King's brother, Richard of Gloucester, arrived in London on May 4, 1483. Immediately he became the focus of many and various plots and counterplots. The Queen's faction clearly wanted to see him stripped of power. Even if Richard of Gloucester was able to maintain his position as Lord Protector, his eventual fate was grim. Two previous Lord Protectors had been executed soon after their charges attained their majority.[29]   Richard probably feared not only for his own life, but also for the lives of his wife and son. His actions in the next three months most likely were at least partially motivated by that fear.

Some time in mid-June, amidst the preparations for young Edward's coronation, Bishop Robert Stillington,[30] visited Richard of Gloucester, and informed the Lord Protector that his brother Edward's marriage to Elizabeth Woodville was canonically invalid.   According to Stillington's account, Edward had betrothed himself to Lady Eleanor Butler.[31]   Later Edward had married Elizabeth Woodville—without first annulling his previous betrothal. If this were true, it would mean that Edward's marriage to Elizabeth had never been legal and that the children born to their union were bastards, and thus unable to inherit the English throne.   It is not known what, if any, evidence Bishop Stillington brough forth to substantiate his story, but whatever it was, Richard chose to believe it. On July 6, 1483, Richard had himself crowned King (as Richard III) in Westminster Cathedral.

Richard III (1452-1485) ruled well for three years. He continued many of his brother Edward's domestic policies, yet his reign was plagued with increasing personal misfortune.   In October, 1483, Richard's cousin, Henry Stafford, the Duke of Buckingham,[31] led a rebellion against his rule. In April of 1484, Richard learned of the sudden death of his eleven year old son. A year later his beloved wife, Anne, died of tuberculosis. Finally, in July, 1485, England was invaded by Henry Tudor (1457-1509),[32] a nephew of Henry VI, and the only remaining heir to the Lancastrian cause. Popular support seems to have been with Richard III, but a desertion among his troops led by Henry's step-father, Thomas, Lord Stanley, led to Richard's defeat and death.

Henry Tudor secured the English throne by marrying Edward IV's eldest daughter, Elizabeth.[33]   Although historically his reign begins the Tudor Age (1485-1603), many Yorkist policies and ideas continued in effect for the next twenty years.

NOTES

[1] Ruled from 1461-1470, and from 1471-1483.

[2] Born 1411. Died 1460.

[3] Born 1421. Died 1471. Ruled from 1422-1460, and 1470-1471.

[4] Henry began to reign when he was only nine months old after the early death of his father Henry V (1387-1422).

[5] Born 1430. Died 1482. Margaret of Anjou was the daughter of Duke Rene of Anjou, and a cousin of the French king. She was married to Henry VI in 1445.

[6] Died 1444.

[7] Richard was the great-grandson of Edward III (1312-1377, reigned 1327-1377), through both his father and his mother. His father, Richard, Earl of Cambridge, was the son of Edward's fourth son, Edmund, while his mother, Anne Mortimer, was descended from the second son, Lionel. King Henry was descended from Edward III's third son, John, so the Yorkist claim that they had more right to the throne since they were descended from an older son has great validity.

[8] For a further discussion of the ambiguity between Queen Margaret and Duke Richard, see chapter 4, "Women in the Wars of the Roses."

[9] *Ingulph's Chronicle of the Abbey of Croyland*, ed. Henry T. Riley (London: George Bell & Sons, 1908), p. 419.

[10] He would later return to his Lancastrian allegiance and be executed after the Battle of Tewkesbury in 1471.

[11]John de Vere lived into the reign of Henry Tudor. He fought for Henry at Bosworth Field (1485).

[12]Born 1437(?). Died 1492.

[13]His birth date is uncertain, but he died in 1471. The Earl inherited his extensive earldom from his wife, Anne Beauchamp. He was a cousin to Edward IV, his father, Richard, having been a brother to Edward's mother, Cecily.

[14]George was executed in 1478; see below.

[15]His death occured in 1483.

[16]*Historie of the Arrivall of King Edward IV*, ed. J. Bruce. (London: Camden Society, 1838), p. 16.

[17]Charles Ross, *Edward IV* (Berkeley: University of California Press, 1974), p. 175. The quote originated in the *Calendar of State Papers* (Milan), vol. I, p. 157.

[18]Cf. Ross, *ibid.*, pp. 351-370, for a detailed discussion of Edward's activities in trade and his laws concerning importing and exporting.

[19]Ross, *ibid.*, p. 352. Original quote is from the *Croyland Chronicle*, but Ross feels that Riley's translation on page 474 is misleading, and so has retranslated it. The quote used here is Ross's translation.

[20]The Treaty of Picquigny, signed on August 15, 1475. Edward promised to give up his claim to the throne of France and betrothed his daughter Elizabeth to the Dauphin Charles.

[21]Dominic Mancini, *The Usurpation of Richard III*; ed. C.A.J. Armstrong (Oxford: Clarendon Press, 1969), pp. 67, 69.

[22]Born 1452. Died 1485.

[23]Born 1456. Died 1485.

[24]Isabel died on December 22, 1476, a few weeks after giving birth. Her death may have been the result of childbirth or it may have been from tuberculosis. The infant was not strong and died a few days later. There never was any evidence that the Duchess or her infant son were poisoned.

[25]Mancini, *op. cit.*, p. 63; cf. Ross, *op. cit.*, pp. 241-243; and, Paul Murray Kendall, *Richard III* (New York: W.W. Norton & Co., 1955), p. 533, for a discussion of Clarence's death.

[26]Mancini, *loc. cit.*.

[27]He never ruled as a crowned monarch, but has been accepted as a king since Tudor historians numbered him as his father's successor.

[28]Mancini, *op. cit.*, p. 71; Kendall, *op. cit.*, p. 193.

[29]Thomas, Duke of Gloucester, was executed by Richard II (1367-1400); and, Humphrey, Duke of Gloucester, who was murdered in 1447.

[30]Bishop of Bath and Wells. He had been chancellor to Edward from 1467 to 1475.

[31]The Duke was Richard's cousin, and was also descended from Edward III. He had been married for ten years to Elizabeth Woodville's sister, Catherine.

[32]Born 1457. Died 1509. See chapter 4, below, "Women in the Wars of the Roses" for more detailed information on his life.

[33]See chapter 2, below, "Marriage." for more details concerning Elizabeth and her marriage to Henry VII.

THE LANCASTER DYNASTY IN ENGLAND

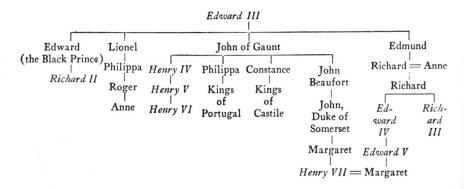

The names of the English kings are italicized. The diagram is extremely simplified.

CHAPTER ONE

Education

Both men and women during the Yorkist Age received a better education than they had during the previous six centuries.[1] In 1405, a statute had been passed in England stating that *"every man or woman of whatever state or condition that he be, shall be free to set son or daughter to take learning on any school that pleases him within the realm."*[2] This statute shows clearly that education was being prized in England and that there were schools available in the country for children to attend. It does not tell, however, how many schools there were or whether or not many people made use of them. Historians assume that schools existed in the larger towns and served the middle class, but the curriculum was not large, probably consisting only of the alphabet, catechism, and religious knowledge.[3] And whether girls even attended these schools is unknown.

It is known that some convents established schools for girls. The curriculum in these schools is also unknown, but Elaine Powers states that we can infer what was taught from what we know about the education of the nuns themselves. The nuns, and probably their secular students, were taught their prayers, songs, spinning, needlework, and probably reading. They may not have been taught how to write.[4]

A Medieval Weaver

Children of the gentry were nearly always sent away from the home in their teens to be educated in the household of someone of their own or higher rank in society. The *Italian Relation*, written during this time period, describes this custom from a foreigner's point of view:[5]

> The want of affection in the English is strongly manifested towards their children. for after having kept them at home till they arrive at the age of 7 or 9 years at the utmost, they put them out, both males and females, to hard service in the houses of other people. . . and few are born who are exempt from this fate, for every one, however rich he may be, sends away his children to the houses of others, whilst he, in return, receives those of strangers into his own. And on enquiring the reason for the severity, they answered that they did it in order that their children might learn better manners.

Finding a suitable position for their children was a major concern for parents. Margaret Paston wrote several letters to her friends trying to find a position for her daughters. An example of such a letter is one written in 1469, to her oldest son, John, asking him to obtain a position for his sister Margery: *"I would ye should purvey for your sister to be with my Lady of Oxford or with my Lady of Bedford or in some other worshipful place. . . ."*[6]

A good position was important because the girl could then bring her family to the notice of her foster parents, and, perhaps, thus obtain their patronage or protection. It was also an excellent way to introduce the young girl to young men of suitable rank and thus contract an advantageous marriage.

Letters of the period indicate the girls were often unhappy in their foster homes. Elizabeth Paston wrote her mother Agnes, complaining of her position, and was told by her mother that *"She must accustom herself to work readily, as other gentlewomen do, and somewhat to help herself therewith."*[7] Dorothy Plumpton wrote several letters to her father, asking to be allowed to come home, but she never received a reply.[8] And yet, as unhappy as these girls were in their foster homes, they probably would have been just as unhappy had they remained with their parents. Discipline during this period was very strict. Beatings and other punishments such as being locked in a room, or going without meals, were common—whether the daughter lived at home or with foster parents. Life during the Yorkist Age was not easy, and children were expected to learn that while they were still young.

The education of these young women was both varied and practical. Primarily they were being trained to be the mistress of a large household. They learned how to manage a home: how much food to lay in to feed their family and the family retainers, how to prepare the food (although few of them would ever prepare food themselves, they had to know how it was done in order to effectively oversee their cooks), where to buy material that they could not produce on their estates, how to supervise servants. They had to learn the art of weaving wool, or, if they were wealthy enough to have someone else do their weaving for them, of sewing and fine needlework. They learned about the care of children. They learn-

A Medieval Baker

ed how to doctor simple illnesses and how to treat war and other wounds. A good deal of time each day was spent learning the social graces: small talk, singing, playing musical instruments such as the lute, dancing, hawking, hunting, chess. In such affluent households which also included male foster children, the girls and boys often spent a couple of hours daily practicing their newly learned social graces upon one another in the presence of a chaperon.[9]

During the Yorkist Age, most women of the upper
and middle classes were taught to read and write English;
some women, especially those of the nobility, also learned
French and Latin. The correspondence of the Age is filled
with letters to and from women. And though it seems that
many, like Margaret Paston, were uncomfortable writing
and employed a secretary, they were able to read fairly
well. Many apparently enjoyed reading, as the number of
books belonging to women attest. Wills of the age show
that many women left psalters, Books of Hours, and other
religious tracts to their heirs. The Duchess Cecily of York,
left several religious books to her granddaughter, Bridgit,
who was a nun. Anne Beauchamp, Duchess of Warwick,
passed her elaborately illustrated *Book of Hours*, a book
which apparently had been commissioned especially for
her by her father, to her daughter, Anne.[10]   Margaret
Beaufort had an extensive library which included several
devotional works in French which she translated into
English in her free time.[11]   Elizabeth Woodville inherited
several devotional works from her husband, Edward IV,
including St. Augustine's *City of God*. Books of fables
and romances were popular, as were the works of Chaucer.
Again, wills of the time indicate which books women read
and owned. Margaret of Anjou enjoyed reading Boccaccio,
and also owned a number of romances, including stories
about Alexander the Great, Charlemagne, Ogier the Dane,
and Guy of Warwick. Her library also held *Le Livre de
Fais Darmes et de Chevalrie*, and *Le Ordre de Gartier*.[13]
Elizabeth Woodville owned the *Romance of the Holy
Grail*, and the *Morte d'Arthur* by Walter Map.[14]   Also
popular with Yorkist women was a French book written
in 1371, and published in English in 1471: *The Book of
the Knight of La Tour Landry*. This was a moralistic
book which gave advice to women on how to properly
live their lives. Finally, it should also be noted, some
women owned copies of John Wycliff's *English Bible*.

Little care was given to Wycliff's work being banned; it was far too popular to put away.[15]

Occasionally women commissioned the writing of a book. *The Beauchamp Pageant*, an illustrated history of the life of Richard Beauchamp, Earl of Warwick (1389-1439), was written some time after 1483, and was probably commissioned by either the late Earl's daughter, Anne Beauchamp, or by his granddaughter, Anne Neville.[16]

Perhaps an indication of how well educated the upper class women were was the interest that these women had in education. Margaret, Duchess of Burgundy, supported the printer William Caxton,[17] and influenced her brother, Edward IV, to become the printer's patron as well. Margaret of Anjou, founded Queen's College, Cambridge, in 1448, and the school was later supported by both Queen Elizabeth Woodville and Queen Anne Neville. Margaret Beaufort endowed the college with a professorship, and persuaded her ward, the Duke of Buckingham, to bestow thirty-one acres of land to the college for its upkeep.[18]

However, although women of the Yorkist Age were better educated than their grandmothers had been, it must be remembered that a university education was denied them. University education in England was still limited to those who sought professions either in law, or in the Church—both of which were closed to women.

Finally, it must be noted that peasant women and domestic servants who were women received little, if any, education. Occasionally a noblewoman would teach her servants some reading, but this was rare—and not socially approved. The peasant woman had neither the leisure nor the inclination for such knowledge. Any education she had was limited to a basic catechism taught by the village priest.[19]

NOTES

[1] During the Middle Ages, only the clergy received an academic education.

[2] Quoted in Eileen Powers, *Medieval Women* (Cambridge: The University Press, 1975), p. 84.

[3] *Ibid.*, pp. 84-85.

[4] *Ibid.*, p. 82.

[5] Quoted in Henry Stanley Bennett, *The Pastons and Their England* (Cambridge: The University Press, 1968 [originally printed in 1922]), p. 82; for the original, see *Italian Relation*, p. 24.

[6] *The Paston Letters*, ed. James Gairdner (London: Camden Society, 1910); letter dated April 3, 1469. Her daughter, Margery Paston had "demeaned" herself by secretly marrying the family steward, Richard Calley. Since she resisted her parent's wishes and had married a man of her own choice, she was never again received by her family. Her lot was easier than another Paston daughter who resisted her parent's demands that she marry their choice, and was, for three moths, "beaten once in a week or twice, sometimes twice in one day, and her head broken in two or three places." Her letters, especially Letter 89, from Margaret Paston to her son, Sir John Paston, spells out her feelings: "My mother and I were with the Lord of Norwich [the bishop], and desired him that he would do no more in the matter of your sister till you and my brothers might be here together. He said plainly that he had been required so often to examine her that he might not nor would no longer delay it. . . and charged that she should be at liberty to come when he sent for her, and he said by his troth that he would be as sorry for her, as if she did not well, as he would if she were right near of his kin, for he knew that her demeaning had stuck sore in our throats. . . . On Friday the bishop sent for her and put her in remembrance how she was born, what kin and friends she had, and should have more if she were ruled and guided by them; and said that he had heard say, that she loved such one that her friends were not pleased with and therefore he bade her be right well advised how she did; and said that he would decide from the words that she had said to him [to Calley], whether it made matrimony or not, and she rehearsed what she had said to him, and said, if those words made it not sure, that she would make it surer, for she said she thought in her conscience she was bound whatsoever the words were. These lewd words grieveth me. . . ." *Original Letters*, ed. J. Fenn (London, 1789), vol. IV, pp. 345-65 for the entire letter.

[7] Gairdner, *op. cit.*, letter 311.

[8] Bennett, *op. cit.*, p. 85.

[9] Powers, *op. cit.*, p. 85.

[10] Pamela Tudor-Craig, *Richard III* (London: Metheun, 1976), pp. 26-27.

[11] E. M. G. Routh, *Lady Margaret: A Memoir of Lady Margaret Beauford, Countess of Richmond and Derby, Mother of Henry VII* (London: Oxford University Press, 1924).

[12] Charles Ross, *op. cit.*, p. 266.

[13] *Ibid.*

[14] *Ibid.*

[15] Paul Murray Kendall, *op. cit.*, p. 386; Pamela Tudor-Craig, *op. cit.*, p. 29.

[16] *Ibid.*, pp. 57-58. The dating of the *Pageant* is based upon the fact that the illustration in the book shows Richard III crowned. Richard was crowned king in 1483.

[17] William Caxton was an English mercer working out of Burges during the years prior to 1470. Sometime between then and 1474, Caxton became interested in the new art of printing. He served an apprenticeship, became a master, and soon began to print books. His first book, printed at Burges in 1474, was dedicated to the Duchess Margaret. When Caxton decided to return to England, Margaret made sure that he had entrance to her brother's court. There, in 1477, he printed the *Dictes and Sayings of the Philosophers* which had been translated by Anthony, Lord Rivers, the brother of Queen Elizabeth. He went on to print editions of Chaucer, Malory, Cicero, Christine de Pisan, and other popular writers. He died in 1491, while working on a translation of *Vitae Patrum*.

[18] Rough, *loc. cit.*.

[19] On the daily life of non-noble women in England who were primarily to be found on farms or estates of large landholders, see, *The Victoria History of Counties of England* (London: Printed for the Society, 1913), 3 volumes. The medieval antecedents to

20

life and labors of common women can be found in Arthur Frederick
Ide, *Special Sisters: Woman in the European Middle Ages* (4th ed.;
Mesquite: Ide House, 1983), pp. 51-68. The only time rural women
were considered equal to rural men, in the eyes of the law, was in
matters concerning physical labor or the payment of fines, bondage,
and the manorial system. See, G. Duby, *Rural Economy and Country Life in the Medieval West*, trans. by C. Posten (London: E.
Arnold, 1968), pp. 485-486; and, *English Economic History*, ed. A.
E. Bland, P. A. Brown, and R. H. Tawney (London, 1930), p. 7.
When the economy slumped with the War of the Roses, women were
legislated against for fear that they were taking the jobs of men; see,
The Little Red Book of Bristol, ed. F. B. Bickley (Bristol, 1900),
vol. II, pp. 127-128.

◆ *The Lancaster and York Dynasties in England** ◆

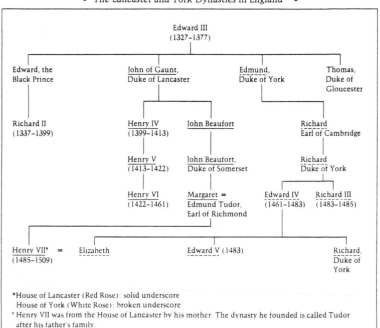

*House of Lancaster (Red Rose): solid underscore
House of York (White Rose): broken underscore
† Henry VII was from the House of Lancaster by his mother. The dynasty he founded is called Tudor
after his father's family.

CHAPTER TWO

Marriage

Marriage was the norm for both men and women in Yorkist society. To remain single was not an option open to most women. Women were either to marry— or to enter a convent. There was no third alternative approved by men—or spoken of by women.

Parents often began searching for a suitable husband for their daughter when the girl was still an infant. The age of consent for girls was twelve,[1] but infant marriages were not unknown. In 1478, six year old Anne Mowbray, heiress to the duchy of Norfolk, married four year old Richard, the younger son of Edward IV.[2] Such marriages of young children usually served a political purpose and are often found among the nobility; seldom are such tender marriages found among the emerging middle class; there is no record of any similar marriage among the poor. Marriages between minors, however, could be repudiated by either party when the minors reached the legal age of consent.[3]

Commoners married later in life than did the gentry. Parents in the upper classes generally betrothed their daughters when the girls were in their teens, if not sooner, and many girls were married and became mothers before they were even twenty years old. Daughters of the merchant class in London and in other large English cities married at a somewhat older age—around twenty or twenty-five, for apprenticeships lasted ten years and both boys and girls were apprenticed to learn a trade.[4] Peasant girls also married later, for they were needed at home to help with household tasks, work in the field, and assist in the rearing of younger brothers and sisters.

Among the gentry, marriage for love during the

Yorkist Age was rare. Arranging a marriage was a matter of business between the fathers of the prospective spouses. A girl was sought after for her dowry, her inheritance, or to unite two families. Because of this business-like attitude toward marriage, the English were often accused of being cold-blooded and heartless by foreign visitors to their country. A Venetian diplomat at the court of Edward IV, declared that: "*I have never noticed anyone, at court or among the lower orders, to be in love. . . .*"[5] Love was expected to grow between a couple after their marriage, but the actual business of finding a marriage partner was based on more practical matters.

Parents during the Yorkist Age chose their daughters' husbands for three basic reasons: to form "blood bonds" or for political alliances, to gain a title, or to increase a fortune. This first basic reason becomes evident when one reads the chronicles of the royal houses of Lancaster and York. The Nevilles, a family related to both royal houses, were especially adept at marrying their daughters to increase their political fortunes. Ralph Neville, the first Earl of Westmoreland, greatly raised his political status when he married Joan Beaufort, the daughter of John, Duke of Lancaster,[6] and the half-sister of King Henry IV. Ralph secured advantageous marriages for his many daughters, including the marriage of Anne to Humphrey Stafford, the Duke of Buckingham; Catherine to John Mowbray, the Duke of Norfolk; and, Cecily, to Richard Plantagenet, the Duke of York.[7] By the third generation, the Nevilles were allied to all the powerful families in the realm and were themselves a power to be reckoned with. Richard Neville, Earl of Warwick ("The Kingmaker"), owed his title to his marriage to Anne Beauchamp,[8] the heiress of Warwick. Because his aunt Cecily Neville had married the Duke of York, Warwick was cousin to the Duke's son, the future King Edward IV. In an effort to expand his power, Warwick offered his two daughters, Isabel and

Anne[9] as wives for Edward's younger brothers: George, Duke of Clarence, and Richard, Duke of Gloucester. Edward refused to sanction the marriages, but George married Isabel Neville in defiance of his brother. Warwick later betrothed his younger daughter, Anne, to Edward of Lancaster, the son of Henry IV, in an effort to effect a reconciliation with the Lancastrian party.[10] The Nevilles indeed were masters at marrying their daughters where it would gain them the greatest political advantage.

During the reigns of the Yorkist kings, only one other family, the Woodvilles, could match the Nevilles in political power, and that family also received a large measure of their prestige through marriage. The Woodvilles supported the House of Lancaster during the first years of the civil war, and were thus out of favor when the eldest daughter of the family, Elizabeth, caught the eye of King Edward. As practical as she was beautiful, Elizabeth refused the king her bed until he married her.[11] After their marriage, and her coronation, Elizabeth used her power as queen to secure advantageous marriages for her two sons from her first marriage, and for her brothers and sisters.[12]

Marriage to form a political alliance was especially important for royal families. A princess knew from childhood that her destiny was to serve her family and her country by marrying a foreign prince. Her duty as wife would be to influence her husband in his dealings with her family and to serve as a peacekeeper between the country of her birth and the country of her marriage. Margaret of Burgundy, the sister of Edward IV, performed this duty admirably. She married Charles, Duke of Burgundy, in 1468, to insure his allegiance to the House of York,[13] and to insure that Burgundy would ally itself with England rather than with France. Almost immediately this alliance proved advantageous, for in 1470, when Edward was forced to flee England, he found refuge at his brother-in-law's court. Charles also loaned Edward money and troops so that he was able to return to England and regain his throne. Margaret continued to support her brothers in England after her husband died. In 1478, she proposed the marriage of her brother George to her step-daughter, Mary, Duchess of Burgundy. King Edward and the Lady Mary herself, however, refused to consider the match.[14]

Margaret continued to serve the interests of the House of York after all three of her brothers had died. After the Battle of Bosworth Field in 1485, she welcomed the Yorkist refugees who fled Henry VII. In 1487, she financially supported the rebellion led by Sir Francis Lovell and John de la Pole, Earl of Lincoln[15] to supplant Henry VII; the rebellion, however, failed. Again, in 1491, she contended that the youth commonly known as Perkin Warbeck was her nephew, Richard of York.[16] Although Warbeck received widespread foreign support and was recognized by several foreign governments as Richard IV, his rebellion also failed and with it ended Margaret's efforts to restore the House of York to the throne of England.

Princess Elizabeth of York would spend the first eighteen years of her life as a pawn in the marriage game. The eldest daughter of Edward IV, she was offered numerous times in marriage. The first time she was offered in marriage occured in 1470, when she was only five years old. The second time, in 1475, she was offered to Dauphin Charles of France. For several years she was referred to as Dauphiness of France, but this betrothal was broken shortly before Edward's death in 1483. Elizabeth spent nearly a year in Westminster Sanctuary following the death of her father, and during that time her mother arranged her betrothal to Henry Tudor, Earl of Richmond, and the Lancastrian claimant to the throne of England. Whether Elizabeth herself consented to this betrothal to an enemy of her house is unknown, but on Christmas Day, 1483, Henry

Tudor publically announced his betrothal to the Princess Elizabeth. The proposed marriage, however, was dependent upon Henry's landing in England, and in successfully overthrowing Richard III. Such an attempt had been made in October, 1483, and had failed. Richard now seemed secure upon his throne. Therefore, in March of 1484, Queen Elizabeth made a deal with Richard whereby he promised that if the princesses left the sanctuary he would

> see that they shall be in surety of their lives and also not suffer any manner hurt. . .nor then nor any of them imprison. . . ; but I shall put them into honest places of good fame, and them honestly and courteously shall see to be founden and entreated, and to have all things requisite and necessary for their exhibitions and findings as my kinswomen; and that I shall do marry [arrange for the marriage of]. . .them to gentlemen born, and every of them give in marriage lands and tenements to the yearly value of 200 marks for the term of their lives. . . . And such gentlemen as shall hap to marry them I shall straitly charge lovingly to love and entreat them, as wives and my kinswomen, as they will avoid and eschew my displeasure.[17]

Elizabeth and her sisters, upon leaving sanctuary, most likely attached themselves to the court of Richard's queen, Anne. During the Christmas season of 1484-5, Elizabeth and Queen Anne appeared in "apparel of identical shape and colour. . . ."[18] This gave rise to the rumor that Richard intended to marry his niece when Anne, who had tuberculosis, died. Richard publically denied the rumor and after Anne's death he sent Elizabeth to his manor of Sheriff Hutton in Yorkshire.

In August, 1485, Henry Tudor invaded England and defeated Richard at the Battle of Bosworth Field. After the battle, he sent for Elizabeth and married her to secure his right to the English throne. History does not record how Elizabeth felt when she finally married a man who had long been considered an enemy of her family. Such marriages were the accepted fate of princesses.

Marriage as a tool to enhance one's political prestige was common among the higher nobility, but among the gentry and middle class, marriage more often became a means of attaining profit and prestige in society. During the Yorkist period, members of the gentry regularly married their daughters into families of wealthy merchants. This had a twofold purpose: the gentry often found themselves land poor and needed the money that marriage into the wealthy business class would bring. Conversely, the members of the business class would see their children attaining what for them was an impossibility: a title. During the Yorkist Age, about one-third of the aldermen of London married into the gentry.[19]

Unfortunately, it was not unknown for a father to sell the marriage of his son or daughter for cash. Here marriage became strictly a business proposition: the father would receive so much money at a specified time if his daughter married the son of a certain tradesman. Although both parents stood to gain by this arrangement, the feelings of the children were not taken into account.

The Paston family of Norfolk epitomizes the Yorkist attitude towards marriage. Their letters contain numerous accounts of how the sons of the house went about the "business" of finding a wife. Especially interesting is the Paston family's treatment of their marriageable daughters.

Elizabeth Paston was locked in her room for three months and "for the most part. . .beaten once in the week or twice, sometimes twice in one day and her head broken in two or three places,"[20] until she agreed to marry Lord Stephen Scrope, a wealthy but infirmed widower more than twice her age. Elizabeth endured her agonies for nothing, for the engagement never came about.

For the next several years the marriage of Elizabeth was a major project in which the entire Paston family participated. Several eligible men were considered and rejected. It was difficult to find a man who was wealthy and who had not been previously married. This was a major consideration, for a previous marriage often meant that he had other children whom he must provide for. The Pastons wanted to insure that whatever lands and money Elizabeth's husband had would go only to Elizabeth and her children after his death, and not be divided between Elizabeth's children and the children of a previous marriage. Finally, when Elizabeth was nearly thirty years old, a suitable husband was found in Richard Poynings. There is no reason to believe that this was a love match, as can be seen from the first letter she wrote to her mother after her marriage: [21]

> As for my master, my best beloved that you call, and I must needs so call now, for I find no other cause, and as I trust in Jesu, none shall; for he is full kind to me. . . .

Women were not only under the control of their father or brothers when it came to marriage, but a woman without a male guardian could be married off by her overlord. Noblemen, or the king, frequently arranged the marriage of their wards for political reasons, without caring to obtain the woman's consent. [22] The sisters of Elizabeth of York, for example, found themselves married to relatives and supporters of Henry VI, after he became king. Catherine Woodville, Dowager Duchess of Buckingham, and sister to Elizabeth Woodville, was married to Henry's uncle and long time supporter, Jasper Tudor. These women had little say in whom they were married to; however, some women without male guardians arranged to pay their overlord a substantial fine for the privilege of choosing their own husband. This worked to the mutual advantage of both the overlord, who often needed the money, and the woman, who could thus protect herself and her property.

Marriage for love, although rare, was not completely unknown in Yorkist England. Town laborers and peasants regularly married the women they loved. A young man looked about his village and chose the girl who appealed to him; he would court her for awhile, and then, with little formality, they would be married. However, even among the peasants it was understood that one did not marry beneath one's social or economic level--and, marriage to combine farms or businesses was not unusual. However, the pressure to make a "suitable" marriage was not as great for the lower classes as it was for the middle class or the gentry.

Occasionally love also had its way among the higher social levels of society. One of the most important marriages of the era was a love match between King Edward IV and Lady Elizabeth Woodville Grey.

Elizabeth was the widow of Sir John Grey, Lord Ferrars, who had been mortally wounded at the Battle of St. Albans. She was left with two young sons to provide for, and was left with little income to do so, for her mother-in-law, Elizabeth Ferrars, denied Elizabeth the right to remain on her husband's property.[23] Elizabeth returned to her parents' home and then turned to their friend and neighbor, William, Lord Hastings, for help. Hastings, a friend and counsellor to King Edward, arranged a meeting between Elizabeth and the King. Legends says that the meeting took place in a clearing, where Elizabeth, holding her two young sons by the hands, cried out to the King for justice as he rode by. The king was impressed by both Elizabeth's beauty and bravery, and agreed to listen to her plea. Over the next few months, he spent more and more time with her at her parents' home of Grafton Regis. Mancini relates that Edward intended to make Elizabeth his mistress, but that even when he put a knife to her throat to force her, she refused.[25] Another chronicler relates that Elizabeth told Edward that she was too good to become his mistress and not good enough to be his queen.[26] Her second statement was certainly true, for although Elizabeth's father was a wealthy lord and her mother was the daughter of the Count of St. Pol, and had, for a time before Henry VI's marriage, been first Lady of England, King Edward was expected to follow the example of his Plantagenet ancestors, and marry a foreign princess. An English lady, no matter how exalted her lineage, would not be considered eligible to become queen. And Elizabeth's lineage was not even exalted. But Edward didn't care. On May 1, 1464, he secretly married the woman he loved. One year later, he had her crowned Queen of England.

Other members of the nobility also managed to marry for love. King James I of Scotland, while being held a prisoner in England, met the king's cousin, Joan Beaufort, and married her. Joan's grandfather and the progenitor of both the Beaufort and the Lancastrian kings, also married the woman he loved, but not until after years of waiting. John, Duke of Lancaster, was the third son of Edward III. As a young man, his parents had arranged his marriage to the Lady Blanche, heiress to the great duchy of Lancaster. Blanche died of the plague several years later. Either shortly before or after her death, John met the Lady Catherine Swynford, and the two fell in love. But Catherine was the daughter of a mere knight, and therefore was not of sufficient rank to marry the king's son. So John married a princess of Castile, and Catherine became his mistress. For twenty years Catherine remained faithful to the Duke, bearing him four children to whom he gave the name of Beaufort. Finally, after the death of his wife, John defied society by marrying the woman he loved. His Beaufort children were legitimated by King Richard II the next year.

Two noblewomen of the Yorkist Age made notorious misalliances when they married men whose social standing was considerably beneath theirs. The first woman, Queen Catherine of Valois, had been married to King Henry V (1387-1422) on June 2, 1419, as a part of a peace treaty between England and France.[27] But Henry died on August 21, 1422, leaving behind a nine month old son and a beautiful widow in her early twenties. Catherine was not allowed to participate in the governing of England, nor was she allowed any influence over how her son was raised. Because of this she retired from court to one of her dower lands and lived a quiet life. Her life was so quiet and she was so removed from the life of the court, that when she met Owen Tudor, fell in love with him, and married him, no one at court was aware that anything had happened. The two lived happily together and had four children[28] before Catherine died in 1437. It was only during her last illness that the news of her second marriage and her second family reached the court.

The second woman who married beneath her social station was Jacquetta, Duchess of Bedford. Jacquetta was the daughter of the Count of St. Pol, and had been married to John, Duke of Bedford. John was the brother of Henry V, and was a much older man than Jacquetta. After his death, the young widowed duchess met and married the handsome Richard Woodville. Although she incurred the wrath of the court and the couple had to pay a substantial fine, the marriage was a happy one which produced seven daughters and five sons.

Although as uncommon among the gentry as it was among the nobility, marriages for love were still managed by some young couples. The story of Margery Paston and Richard Calley shows how love can make an ordinarily obedient young woman determined to have her own way, no matter what the consequences. Margery was the youngest daughter of Margaret and John Paston, Esquire, and like the other daughters of the family, she found herself the object of various matrimonial plans. But Margery had plans of her own. She fell in love with the Paston's chief baliff, Richard Calley, and the two became secretly betrothed. Margery kept their love a secret for awhile, knowing that her family would strongly disapprove of her marriage to anyone of a lower social standing than herself. When the family did learn of the attraction between the two young people, they kept the lovers apart. For two years Margery and Richard never saw one another, and rarely did they communicate. But their love remained strong, as is shown in a letter written to Margery by Richard at the end of that period:[29]

> Mine own lady and mistress, and before God very true wife, I with heart sorrowful recommend me unto you, as he that cannot be merry, nor naught shall be till it be otherwise with us than it is yet, for this life that we lead now is neither pleasure to God nor to the world, considering the great bond of matrimony that is made betwixt us, and also the great love that hath been and as I trust yet is betwixt us, and as on my part never great; wherefore I beseech Almighty God comfort us as soon as it pleaseth Him, for we that ought of very right to be most together are most asunder, me seemeth it a thousand year ago since I spoke to you, I had lever than all the good in the world I might be with you. . . .

Soon after the receipt of this letter, Margery informed her family of their betrothal. Because a betrothal was as binding as a marriage and could only be broken by an annulment, the Pastons tried to deny that it had ever taken place. They urged Margery to deny it, but she refused. Finally, both she and Richard Calley were examined by Walter Lyhert, Bishop of Norwich, to see if there was any flaw in the betrothal. When Margery came before him "she rehearsed what she had said [to Richard Calley], and said if these words made it [the betrothal] not sure, she said boldly that she would make it surer ere she went thence, for she said she thought in her conscience she was bound whatever the words were. . . ."[30]   Upon hearing this, the bishop regretfully decided that the betrothal between Margery Paston and Richard Calley was indeed legitimate, and that they could no longer be kept apart. When she learned of the bishop's decision, Margaret Paston ordered her servants "that she [Margery] should not be received in my house."[31]   Her daughter was lodged with acquaintances of the bishop until her marriage. Apparently the Paston family eventually reconciled themselves to the marriage, for Richard Calley remained chief baliff and Margery's children were remembered in her mother's will.

Love was more common between husband and wife after the marriage had been performed, than before the marriage was consecrated. During the Yorkist Age, one sees that many marriages conceived for political or monetary benefit later became love matches between husband and wife. Such a marriage, apparently, was that between Richard, Duke of Glouchester, and Anne Neville. Anne and Richard were cousins and had known one another from childhood, but their paths had diverged when Anne's father, the Earl of Warwick, quarreled with Richard's brother, Edward IV. Anne fled with her family to France where her father betrothed her to Edward of Lancaster, the son of Queen Margaret of Anjou. After the battles of Barnet and Tewkesbury, where both the Earl and the young prince Edward died, Richard tried to seek Anne out. But George, Duke of Clarence, claimed wardship over the girl by right of his marriage to Anne's sister, Isabel, and refused to let anyone see her. When Richard persisted, obtaining royal permission to call on the girl, Clarence replied that he had no knowledge of Anne's whereabout. The author of the *Croyland Chronicle* relates:[32]

> [Clarence] caused the damsel [Anne] to be concealed in order that it might not be known by his brother where she was; as he was afraid of the division of the Earl [Warwick's] property, and wished to come to himself alone in right of his wife and not be obliged to share it with any other person. Still, however, the craftiness of the Duke of Gloucester so far prevailed, that he discovered the young lady in the city of London disguised in the habit of a cookmaid; upon which he had her removed to the sanctuary of St. Martin's.

Some historians have either made Richard the hero, or the villain of the story. Probably he was neither. Anne was an astute young lady; she knew that she was a great heiress and undoubtedly didn't want her half of her heritage to go to her greedy brother-in-law. She also knew that she had to marry again and she knew that Richard was the only unmarried man in England who was both her social equal and strong enough to protect her and her lands.[33] She undoubtedly chose the match for practical reasons. However, it should be remembered that Richard and Anne had grown up together at her father's castle of Middleham, they knew one another, and probably got along well together. It is possible, as some historians and many novelists have postulated, that Richard and Anne were in love.

The Duke of Clarence strongly opposed the marriage between his brother and sister-in-law. A battle between the brothers ensued which ended only when Richard agreed to accept less than half of Anne's inheritance and to relinquish his title of Great Chamberlain of England to Clarence.

Richard and Anne were married sometime after Easter of 1472, and left immediately afterwards for their castle of Middleham, near York. Their marriage was a happy one, as related by Kendall:[34]

> . . .Richard's marriage was happy. . .he gave Anne Neville his heart as well as his name. Even the Tudor historians, for all their zest in elaborating monstrous

legends of Richard's wickedness, cast no slur upon his
marital fidelity, and Mancini gives positive testimony
that the purity of his private life was well known to the
public.

Anne also appears to have been devoted to her husband. She supported his ambitions and traveled with him
whenever he left Middleham on business for the king (except, of course, for the times he went to war). That their
marriage was a loving one is testified to by Richard's deep
grief when Anne died of tuberculosis at the young age of
twenty-nine.[35]

What was it like for the Yorkist woman once she was
married? Legally, she became the property of her husband. Although we have seen instances where wives were
greatly loved by the men they married, and we will see, in
a later chapter, women who were nearly the equals of their
husbands in business or politics, nevertheless, legally they
were a man's inferior.

Except in rare cases, when a woman married any
property she brought to the marriage became her husband's to manage. Generally he could do as he wished
with it, although if he divorced her, he was obligated to
return to her the full value of the property which she
brought to the marriage.[36] That the husband had full
control over his wife's property is seen clearly in a pro-
nouncement by the first Parliament of Henry VII, which
gave Henry's mother, Margaret Beaufort, the right to
manage her property as if she were not married.[37] When
a husband died, if the couple had been childless, the
property reverted to the wife to dispose of as she pleased.
If there had been children of the marriage, the property
of both husband and wife went to them, with the wife
retaining only one-third of the whole as her dower lands.
These were for her use during the remainder of her life,

but reverted back to the estate when she died.

Legally, a woman remained a minor her entire life. She could not, with rare exceptions,[38] go to court on her own behalf; her husband must appear with her. A sixteenth century law, similar to the laws of the time, reads as follows:[39]

> Every Feme Covert [married woman] is a sort of infant . . . .It is seldom, almost never that a married woman can have any action to use her wit only in her own name; her husband is her stern, her prime mover, without him she cannot do much at home, and less abroad. . . .It is a miracle that a wife should commit any suit without her husband.

and:[40]

> The very goods which a man giveth to his wife, are still his own, her chain, her bracelets, her apparel, are all the goodman's goods. . . .A wife however gallant soever she be, glitterth but in the riches of her husband, as the moon hath no light but it is the sun's. . . . For thus it is, if before marriage the woman was possessed of horses . . . .sheep, corn, wool, money, plate and jewels, all manner of movable substance is presently . . . the husband's to sell, keep or bequeath if she died.

The ideal wife was someone who was patient, softspoken, a good housewife, and above all, obedient. Powers quotes the Managier de Paris who compares a good wife to a faithful dog: someone who obeys all her husband's orders, whether they are just or unjust, important or not, reasonable or unreasonable.[41] A woman who did not obey her husband could be beaten, either with the hands or with staves. Even Canon Law allowed for this!

Although the Church condemned adultery, in an age when the vast majority of marriages were arranged between couples who met shortly before or at their wedding, it is not surprising that a large number of men and women took lovers. Women were more discreet than men in their adulterous affairs, for they had more to lose should they be discovered. The Managier de Paris advises women:[42]

> Every good quality is obscured in the . . . woman whose virginity falters. . . .This is why women of sense avoid not only the sin itself but also the appearance of it, so as to keep the good name of virginity. . . .Know too that riches, beauty, and all other virtues are lost and as nothing in the woman so stained. For a woman need only once be suspected for all to be utterly . . . lost, ruined and effaced without hope of recovery . . . . So you see in what peril a woman places her honor and that of her husband's lineage and of her children when she does not avoid the risk of such blame.

Women caught in adultery could be forced to do public penance, as Jane Shore was for her long affair with Edward IV. A man could divorce his adulterous wife and keep for himself any lands or wealth she had brought to the marriage.

NOTES

[1]Powers, *op. cit.*, p. 40.

[2]Anne died in 1481, a few days before her tenth birthday. By an unusual clause in the marriage contract, her lands, which normally should have gone to her cousin, John Howard, instead remained the property of the young Richard.

[3]Powers, *loc. cit.*.

[4]Paul Murray Kendall, *The Yorkist Age* (London: Allen & Unwin, 1962), p. 372. For more detail on apprenticeship, see chapter 3, below.

[5]Kendall, *ibid.*, p. 371.

[6]The Beauforts were children by John and his third wife, Catherine Swynford. Catherine had been the Duke's mistress for several years before they married, and the children were all illegitimate. However, after their marriage, King Richard II legitimatized his cousins as a favor to his uncle.

[7]J. R. Lander, *Crown and Nobility, 1450-1509* (London: Edwin Arnold; Montreal: McGill-Queen's University Press, 1976), pp. 95-97.

[8]Anne and her brother Henry were the only heirs of Richard Beauchamp, Earl of Warwick. Both were married to children of Richard Neville. When Henry died, the entire inheritance devolved upon Anne and through her to her husband, Richard Neville, who became Earl of Warwick.

[9]Warwick's daughters, Isabel and Anne, were co-heiresses to his great fortune.

[10]The betrothal took place and a dispensation to marry (they were cousins) was obtained from the Patriarch of Jerusalem, but it is not known if the marriage ever took place. It is possible that both Warwick and Queen Margaret wished to wait until Henry was secure upon the English throne for the marriage to be consummated. If their scheme failed, it would be much easier for Anne and Edward to get an annulment if the marriage had never actually taken place or been consummated.

[11]Mancini, *op. cit.*, p. 61.

[12]Lander, *op. cit.*, p. 110-114; Ross, *op. cit.*, pp. 93-94.

[13]The Burgundian Ducal House had previously supported Margaret of Anjou.

[14]The fear of both parties was that Clarence would use the Duchy of Burgundy as a stepping-stone to the English throne. Also, Mary needed a strong husband who could protect her lands from the French. She ultimately married the Holy Roman Emperor, Maximilian (1459-1519).

[15]Francis, Lord Lovell, was a close friend of Richard's from the days when they had both been wards of the Earl of Warwick. John de la Pole was the son of Richard's sister Elizabeth, Duchess of Suffolk, and had been Richard's heir after the death of his son, Edward. Both men died in the rebellion.

[16]See chapter 4, below, for more detail on Margaret's involvement in Warbeck's attempt to secure the English throne.

[17]Harlein MS 433.

[18]*Croyland Chronicle*, p. 572.

[19]During the reign of the Tudor monarchs, many members of the nobility could trace themselves back to such marriages. Anne Boleyn's grandfather had been a mercer in London who married a noblewoman. Her father had married the daughter of the Duke of Norfolk. Anne (1507-1536) herself would become Queen of England.

[20]Although such treatment happened, Gairdner, in his introduction to the *Paston Letters*, comments that it was very rare and only happened in cases where the parents were severely displeased with their daughters.

[21]*Paston Letters*; see footnote 6, p. 18, above.

[22]Powers, *loc. cit.*.

[23]Landers, *op. cit.*, p. 106.

[24]There was such a preserve in Northamptonshire near the Woodville residence of Grafton Regis.

[25]Mancini, *loc. cit.*.

[26]See *The Issue of Station in the Lives of English Nobles, 1066-1503*, ed. J. A. Rawlinton (Saskatoon: Gill House, 1902), p. 123.

[27]The Treaty of Troyes, proclaimed May 21, 1419. This provided that when the king, Charles VI, was incapable of ruling, Henry was to be made regent and heir.

[28]According to Vergil. The two oldest sons were Jasper Tudor, later Earl of Pembroke, and Edmund Tudor, later Earl of Richmond and father of Henry VII. A younger son became a monk and died young, while the daughter became a nun. Their names are unrecorded.

[29]*Paston Letters, loc. cit.*.

[30]*Ibid.*

[31] *Ibid.*

[32] *Croyland Chronicel*, pp. 469-470.

[33] Ross, *op. cit.*, p. 28. He goes into greater detail on this theory.

[34] Kendall, *Richard III*, p. 34.

[35] The stories that Richard poisoned his wife are found in some of the Tudor chronicles; they are mere fabrications. Anne was ill in December and indications are that she had been ill as early as October. Although there are contemporary indications in the *Croyland Chronicle* that Richard considered marrying his niece Elizabeth, after his wife's death, there are no contemporary indications that Richard wished Anne dead.

[36] Powers, *op. cit.*, p. 38.

[37] Rough, *op. cit.*, p. 58; see chapter 4, below, for quotes from the original document.

[38] Some exceptions are given in chapter 3, below.

[39] *The Lawes Resolutions of Women's Rights*, late 16th century compilation by the anonymous T. E. (London, 1632), pp. 141, 204; quoted in *Not in God's Image*, ed. Julia Faolin and Laura Martines (New York: Harper and Row, 1973), p. 145.

[40] *The Lawes Resolutions of Women's Rights*, pp. 129ff; as cited in *Not in God's Image*, p. 149.

[41] Power, *op. cit.*, p. 16.

[42] *Le Managier de Paris*, 1393; quoted in *Not in God's Image*, pp. 141-142.

Perpendicular Gothic at Lincoln

York Minster

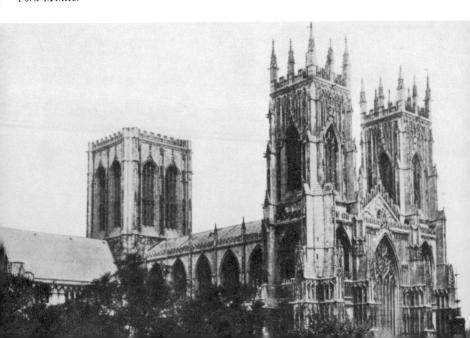

CHAPTER THREE

Daily Life

The woman of the Yorkist Age was predominately a housewife. Regardless of whether she was a duchess, a merchant, or a peasant, her primary responsibility was to oversee the household: lay in supplies, cook (or oversee the cooking), supervise servants and apprentices, and care for the children (both her own, and those who were placed under her care and direction). Other duties may have been important, and they may at times have superceded housewifery, but if a woman failed at managing her household, she was considered a failure in all things. A Yorkist woman's education was geared towards one thing: to be an efficient housekeeper. And with very few and rare exceptions, that is what all Yorkist women were.[1]

The Gentry

A Lady in Yorkist England had the immense task of overseeing at least one, and probably more than one, manor or estate. She was personally responsible for all those living on the manor, not just her immediate family, but also her husband's retainers, wards, foster children, men-at-arms, and servants. In a large household, like that of the Earl of Warwick, or the Duke of Clarence, this could include some two thousand people. More usually, however, it averaged around a hundred persons. The gentlewoman arranged food and accommodations for this large crowd. She hired the servants and oversaw their work. She dealt with merchants and tradesmen. She personally tended the herb garden and saw that the family's domestic animals were cared for. It was a busy life, but as we have seen, it was one for which she was well prepared.[2]

Provisioning the household with food was perhaps the largest task that the gentlewoman had to face. Most food-stuffs used on the manor were grown or prepared on the lands. The Lady of the manor had to insure that enough food was retained for the family's use before the surplus could be sold. Under or over estimating could be a serious mistake, for too little food reserved could mean that people would starve, and too much food meant that supplies would spoil.

The manor or castle was a small society of its own. Most manors had a brewery, bakehouse, herb garden, and a dairy. Enormous amounts of food were consumed at each meal, and the gentlewoman had to insure that there was always enough for everyone, with little left over since there was no way to store or preserve it. Under her supervision, bread was baked daily in the bakehouse: white bread for the gentry, and a coarser bread for the servants. Ale was brewed in the brewhouse; butter and cheese made in the dairy. In the larder candles were made, bacon cured and meat salted down for the long winter when fresh food was scarce. The herb garden supplied seasonings for the food, especially important during the winter months of salted meat, as well as herbs for home medicinal remedies. Other household necessities such as spices, wine, fish for Lent, had to be ordered from merchants. Many of these were available only in the larger cities such as London or York, making it important that the Lady keep a good accounting of what supplies she was low on so that one trip to the city could suffice to obtain all the needed goods.[3] The Paston letters contain many requests for needed victuals and other supplies. One year the bailiff wrote Margaret Paston concerning the ordering of fish for Lent:[4]

> Mistress, it were good to remember your stuff of herring now this fishing time. I have got me a friend in Lowes-

toft to help me buy seven or eight barrell and [they]
shall not cost me above 6/8s a barrell. . . . You shall do
more now [Autumn] with 40 shillings than you shall
do at Christmas with five marks.

Other letters contain requests for pots of treacle, sugar
loaves, spices such as pepper, cloves, mace, ginger, cinna-
mon, and saffron, and exotic fruits such as oranges, dates,
and almonds.

The making of cloth and clothing was another important task for the Yorkist gentlewoman. Although by
the middle of the fifteenth century the weaving industry
was expanding in England, many women still spun and
wove at least a portion of their cloth at home. Women of
the lower classes spent a good deal of time in this pursuit,
setting up looms before the fire or out of doors during the
summer months to work on the seemingly endless supply
of cloth needed for the family. The gentry were able to
hire young women to come and weave their cloth for them
or were able to buy ready-made cloth from London and
other major cities. Experienced seamstresses worked long
hours in many manors making cloth and cutting clothes
for the lord and lady, their children, their retainers and
servants. But women like Margaret Paston still attempted
to do some of the family sewing in their free time, as is
seen in this letter to one of her sons:[5]

I should have got them [some shirts] made up here, but
that should have been too long ere you should have
them. Your aunt or some other good woman will do. . .
them.

The cloth that was produced on the manor was usually
woven from wool obtained from the manor's sheep. Luxurious cloths such as silks and velvets were imported and
usually had to be bought in the larger towns, as did cloth
of any unusual color.[6]

Purchased or woven cloth was made up into clothing. English women of the Yorkist Age loved rich materials, and exciting colors in their gowns. Dresses were worn long, often with longer trains flowing behind them. The waistline was raised to just beneath the breasts, and was belted with a wide, jeweled belt. Sleeves were either loose and flowing, or fitted and very long. Married women always wore their hair covered. While at home they might wear a simple veil or wimple, but at other times, heavy, elaborate head-dresses were worn. The tall, elaborate henin (made popular as head-dresses worn by princesses in fairy tale illustrations) was popular on the continent, but it does not seem to have caught on in England. When English women did wear it, they shortened it, and squared off the end, making it lighter and more comfortable to wear. Much more popular than the henin was the butterfly head-dress which consisted of a wire frame shaped like wings from which gauze was drapped. Both of these head-dresses entirely covered the hair. Any hair on the forehead that was left exposed was often plucked out, the mode of the day being to seem to have a high forehead.

The gentlewoman of Yorkist England lived in considerable more comfort than her grandmother. Although when on her estates she may reside in a castle that had been built a hundred years earlier, many of these castles had new additions which made them more comfortable than the draughty, dark, older fortresses had been. Castles were used less for defense and more for homes. Windows were no longer small and narrow, to be used primarily for defense, but were large enough to let in adequate light, and many were even plated with clear or colored glass. Richard III added a new hall to his castle at Middleham which was smaller and less prone to drafts than the original had been. He also modernized his castles at Sudely, Sheriff Hutton, and Warwick. The Pastons removed the drawbridge from their manor at Gresham and replaced it with a causeway lined with hedges. All of these additions were to make old, uncomfortable manors more liveable and modern.

The townhouses of the gentry and merchant classes were considerably more comfortable than the ancient manors were. Such houses were often large, with numerous bedrooms so that members of the family and their guests could have privacy, something unheard of in the days when everyone slept in the same bedchamber with the guests bedded with the servants in the great hall! Solars were built in many of the newer homes so that the family could spend some time in privacy rather than in the great hall with the servants. Usually these solars were well lit rooms with fireplaces in the walls and tiled floors which may have been covered with carpets rather than the more traditional rushes. Furniture was still sparse, as it had been thoughout the Middle Ages. Houses contained few chairs; women and children usually sat on stools or on cushions piled on the floor. Trestle tables and benches were still used to eat from in most homes. Beds were large and comfortable, at least for the master and mistress, but servants and sometimes children, slept on pallets on the floor.[7]

The Yorkist woman was responsible for caring for this house. She was also the representative of her husband when he was unavailable. She was prepared to take over the complete business of running the estate when her husband was away on business, or at war. Women, like Margaret Paston, defended their property against invaders, initiated lawsuits, and negotiated with the tenants. Christine de Pisan notes:[8]

> Because that knights, esquires, and gentlemen go upon journeys and follow the wars, it beseemeth wives to be wise and of great governance and to see clear, in all that they do, for that most often they dwell at home without their husbands who are at court or in divers lands.

Elaine Powers, in her book *Medieval Women*, continues:[9]

> A Lady must be skilled in the niceties of tenure and
> feudal law, in case the lord's rights were invaded; she
> must know all about the management of the estate, so as
> to supervise the bailiff. . . .

Prof. Ide, in his chapter "Women and the Defense of the
Land," writes:[10]

> Medieval European [and English] women were ac-
> customed to war. Each expected to fight when neces-
> sary—fighting beside their men in defense of hearth and
> home. Not only were they expected to weild weapons
> beside their husbands, fathers, and brothers, but if the
> male head of the house was gone on pilgrimage, to
> market, to court, or on any other journey, and the
> house or property was attacked, each one was expected
> to defend the cradle, caldron, and covenant, as would
> the English Countess Buchanan when her leige king
> Edward I demanded she surrender her husband's castle
> of Berwick in the thirteenth century; and, as later oc-
> cured in 1338, when Black Agnes, Countess of Dunbar,
> singlehandedly fought back the encroachments and
> hegemonic aspirations of King Edward III; or, as Alice
> Knyvet did when she repelled the advances of Edward
> IV in 1461, when that British monarch attempted to
> storm her refuge: Bokenham Castle.

Some women oversaw the management of their own
lands regardless of whether or not their husbands were
available. Agnes Paston retained control over the lands
she inherited without interference from either her husband
or her sons. Her son often collected rents for her, but she
always knew exactly what was due her, as is attested to by
this letter:[11]

> I pray you, forget not to bring me my money from Harl-
> ingbury, as you come from London—either all or a great
> part. The debt was due this Christmas last past. . .and at
> midsummer it is 15 more. . . .

Not all women remained behind to administer the estates when their husbands left home. Many accompanied their husbands as they traveled on business. Duchess Cecily of York nearly always accompanied her husband, as can be seen from the birthplaces of her children: Anne at Northampton, Henry at Hatfield, Edward and Edmund at Rouen, France, Margaret at Northampton, John at Westminster, George at Dublin, and finally, Richard at Northampton.[12] Anne Neville traveled with her husband, Richard of Gloucester; records show that she spent the feasts of Christmas, Lent, Easter, and Corpus Christi, with him in York nearly every year during the twelve years they resided at Middleham—the only exceptions being the years they traveled south to spend the holidays at King Edward's court.[13] Later, when she became queen, Anne continued to accompany her husband, a rarity for a Medieval queen who usually traveled separate from her husband.

Many women enjoyed occasional travel. During most of the year the lady was isolated on her estates with no one of her own rank nearby. But at least once a year most families traveled to London or some other large city. There the gentlewoman could renew her friendships with other women of her class. Margaret Paston mentions in several letters to her husband that she spent a pleasant day visiting with her good friend, Elizabeth Clare. Entire afternoons could be spent catching up on the news which they had not had a chance to exchange for six months or more.

Yorkist women enjoyed several different activities in their spare time. As has been mentioned previously, many women were literate and spent their time reading religious tracts or romances. Even women who were not literate enjoyed being read to while they sewed or did needlework. Needlework was a major pastime; women embroidered designs on clothes, table linen or linen for the chapel. Hunting and hawking, a necessity during the winter if one did not wish to subsist only on salted meat, was also enjoyed by many ladies.

The Merchant/Middle Class

While women of the gentry were primarily house-
wives, the middle class woman was often both housewife
and business woman. It was not unusual for a middle class
woman to begin working when she was a child and con-
tinue into old age. Some women even became wealthy as
a result of their labors.

The average middle class woman rose before daybreak
to prepare, perhaps with the help of a serving girl or ap-
prentice, a breakfast of bread, ale, meat and cheese, for her
family and her husband's apprentices. When everyone had
finished, and the dishes had been cleared from the table,
washed, and put away, she joined her husband at his work
or she set off for her own place of employment.

The majority of tradeswomen worked side by side
with their husbands. That women were considered to be
competent to do a man's work or to run a business is testified to in the number of wills in which men left their
entire business to their wives when they died. The guilds
had laws which specifically allowed women to carry on
their husband's trade, although the women themselves
were seldom allowed to join the guild.[14]

Assisting her husband was not the only option available to women during the Yorkist Age. Many women,
both married and single, ran their own businesses. It
was not unusual for a woman to be apprenticed to a trade
when she was a young girl, as many wills of the period
attest.

A good number of women seem to have remained
independent businesswomen even after their marriage. The
law continued to recognize those women as independent
entrepreneurs, totally separate from their husbands. Their

husbands were not responsible for any of their successes or failures in business, and if the wife broke the law, the husband was not punished for it:[15]

> Where a woman coverte de baron [married] follows any craft within the said city by herself apart, with which the husband in no way intermeddles, such a woman should be bound as a single woman in a Court of Record, she shall have her law and other advantages byway of plea just as a single woman. And if she is condemned she shall be committed to prison until she shall have made satisfaction; neither the husband nor his goods shall in such case be charged or interfered with.

What forms of work did Yorkist women take part in? Elaine Powers notes that women worked as butchers, chandlers, ironmongers, netmakers, shoemakers, glovers, haberdashers, pursemakers, capmakers, skinners, bookbinders, gilders, painters, spicers, smiths, and goldsmiths. Some dealt with trade and exporting.[16] The silk-weaving industry was almost entirely in the hands of women. Many women who entered this line of work seem to have become extremely successful in it. Edward IV patronized one woman exclusively when he needed silk tassals for his books. Another young woman, Agnes Langton, was successful enough to sell her silk throughout England. When she died young, she left business debts of £300; her mother, who took over the business, was easily able to discharge the debt from the profits, and continued to make the business a success. Other women during the Yorkist Age, especially women in London, had a monopoly on the business of embroidering and embellishing cloth with jewels.

Although many women of the middle class worked outside the home, they definitely were not considered as equals to men. Women were banned from the professions of law, medicine, clergy, and government. They could not attend the universities. Women were rarely admitted as full members of the guilds, and those few women who were admitted were almost always the wives or widows of male members. Crafts monopolized by women, such as silkweaving, did not even have a guild. Laws were passed which restricted the work which women were allowed to do. A London law, similar to ones passed in other cities, forbade women other than the wives and daughters of craftsmen, to work for pay. Men rationalized that women were too frail to work, but the real reason for banning women from the crafts becomes evident when one reads the following complaint made by the weavers of Bristol in 1461:[18]

> . . .by the which many and diverse of the King's liege people, likely men to do the king's service in his wars and defense of the land and sufficiently learned in said craft goeth vagrant and unoccupied and may not have their labour to their living. . .

women weavers take jobs away from men!

More important to many families than a regular job, were the bye-industries—jobs which women did from their home to supplement the family income. Probably the majority of middle class women were involved in some way with a bye industry. In their spare time women would brew ale, bake bread, spin wool, weave cloth, keep a tavern, make or sell charcoal. Many women even had more than one industry going at the same time—for example, she might bake bread and brew ale. Other women limited themselves to selling excess produce from their garden.

The chief bye industry during the Yorkist Age was the spinning of wool. During the later part of the fifteenth century, the wool trade was expanding. More and more women bought ready-made cloth rather than spinning their own. This necessitated the employment of large numbers of people to spin and weave the wool. Men did most of the weaving, but their wives and daughters spun the wool for them. This was a job which could be done in the evenings while sitting in front of the fire; it did not take time away from the many other jobs which a woman had to do during the day.

The Yorkist Age was an age of improving lifestyle for the members of the middle class since both Edward IV and Richard III encouraged trade. The middle class, which two centuries earlier had barely existed, now often rivaled the nobility in wealth and influence. Even the lower levels of the middle class–the common laborers and small shop owners–were fairly prosperous during this period.

The wealth of the middle class showed in their homes and their clothing. The Yorkist women presided over a house that was larger and more comfortable than the one their grandmothers had lived in. Like the town houses of the nobility, the middle class house had a private solar for the family, as well as individual bedrooms. Most residences had small gardens. Some of these homes were so luxurious that members of the nobility rented them when they stayed in town. Kendall describes the residence of Stephen Browne, grocer and twice mayor of London:[19]

> his residence had oak-paneled hall, 40 by 24 feet, running north and south, and was entered from the court by a flight of stone steps. As in most houses of this kind. . . the buttery, pantry, and kitchen, lying to the north were screened off from the hall. . .while an entry from the south end led to a series of family chambers, including the chapel.

Kendall comments that the house took up an entire city block.

Clothing worn by the middle class was more elegant even than their homes. They could afford to buy clothes of the same material and richness as the nobility, and they saw no reason to deny themselves. A sumptuary law was passed in 1461, forbidding the use of materials such as velvet and cloth of gold, as well as the use of certain colors by the middle class: "because the commons of this Realm do daily wear excessive and inordinate array to the great displeasure of God"[20], but such sumptuary laws were almost impossible to enforce, and so the middle class in Yorkist England continued wearing velvets, jewels, sable and gold.

The Peasant

The lives of peasant women had not improved much since the beginning of the Middle Ages. Although the majority were now free and no longer serfs bound to serve the lord of the manor, their daily life was still much the same as it had been for the last three centuries.

Most peasants lived in small villages still associated with the manor. The peasants farmed land owned by the manor lord and paid him a yearly rent. Their life was hard, for most peasants had few acres to farm and in a year of either drought or excessive rain, starvation killed a good portion of the peasant population—taking especially the sick, old, the very young, and pregnant or nursing women.

On their land the peasants of Yorkist England grew wheat and barley which they used for their own consumption, or sold it at market fairs.[21] Most peasants also kept sheep and cattle which were grazed on the common land,[22] for sheep were needed for wool which clothed the family; cattle were also maintained for their milk, cheese, butter, and cream.[23]

Peasant women worked harder than women in the other social classes of Yorkist society. Their day began before dawn. After feeding the animals and preparing breakfast for the husband and children of the house, the individual Yorkist peasant woman worked along side of her men in the fields, planting and harvesting as the seasons dictated. When not occupied with harvesting or planting the peasant woman spent her time cultivating her own private vegetable garden, making cheese and butter, spinning wool, sewing clothes, baking bread, preparing meals, brewing ale, making candles and soap, and caring for children. Many peasant women were also involved in the bye industries mentioned earlier in this chapter. Oftentimes they produced more than the quantity of supplies needed by their families, and could sell the extra bread, butter, cheese, or vegetables at market. Some peasant women also kept bees and sold the honey. Others set themselves up as tavern-keepers and brewers of ale for public consumption.[24]

Life was hard for the peasant woman, and many peasant women died young. Pregnancy and child-bearing were leading causes of death among young peasant women. There was no effective birth control methods available, and village priests and visiting bishops denounced those women who "did that which is unnatural"—practice any form of birth control, that many women bore one child after another—often bearing a child every eighteen months or so after her marriage at the age of thirteen or fourteen. It is no wonder that women of twenty-five died, exhausted from the rigours of bearing and caring for so many children. Dorothy Hartley, in *Lost Country Life*, notes:[25]

The Medieval midwife. . .would note that a child conceived in autumn and carried through the dark months of sparse diet when there was no meat, no milk, nor eggs, nor green food, was likely to be a poor baby at birth; but if it survived it would have the good spring and summer foods, and sunshine and warmth for its first year of growth. Whereas a baby conceived in spring and carried through the summer months was likely to be a fine bonny baby at birth, but to lose badly during its first winter. Seeing this, they may well have noted the variations in diet during pregnancy, the extra salt of winter dried meat, for they advised the mother to get a kiddle goat late, to provide a late supply of milk, and to keep some beast alive to be slaughtered as late as possible. They were always anxious to satisfy the food whim of a pregnant woman, considering it important to her welfare.

The dwellings of the peasant changed little over the past two centuries. Most peasants lived in a small wooden house which contained only one or two rooms and perhaps a loft. Most of these houses had fireplaces of some type, but few had chimneys, so they were incredibly smokey whenever a fire was going. The kitchen if the house had a separate kitchen, was in a detached from the rest of the dwelling.

The peasant's home held little furniture. The peasant usually owned only a few stools, benches, a chest for storage, perhaps a table.[26] Some peasants appear to have been fairly well off, for in their wills they leave pewter and iron utensils, silver spoons, belts of silver and furniture such as beds, tables, and chairs.[27]

Life for the peasant woman was not all work and drudgery. Feast days were scattered throughout the year, and on those days, the woman enjoyed herself along with her neighbors. However, even on feast days, she had her work to do, as is so graphically described in this fifteenth century poem:[28]

The Farmer's Feast Day

Good huswives whom God hath enriched enough,
forget not the feasts that belong to the plow,
the meaning is onely to joy and be glad,
for comfort with labour would sometime be had.

Shrovetide
At Shrovetide to shroving go thresh the fatte henne,

if blindefilde can kill it then geve it thy menne.
Maides fritters and pancakes inough see ye make,
let slutte have one pancake for caompanys sake.

Sheepshearing
Wife make us feast, spare fleshe neither corne
make Wafers and cakes, for our shepe must be shorne.
At sheep shearing neighbors no other thing crave
but good chere and welcome like neighbors to have.

The Wake Day
To Oven with the flawns mayd, passe not for slepe,
to-morrow thy father his wake day shal kepe;
then grimly go daunce with what Lover ye will,
though love make you beaten, kepe Lover yet still.

Harvest Home
For all this good feasting yet are thou not loose
til thou give the Ploughman in harvest his goose,
though goose go in stubble, yet passe not for that,
let goose have a goose be shee leane be shee fat.

The major feast of the year was Christmas and the wife prepared for the season months ahead of time. It was a time of feasting and gaity for all levels of society.

Christmas Husbandly Fare[29]

Good husband and huswife, now chiefly be glad
things handsome to have, as they ought to be had.
They both do provide, against Christmas do come,
to welcom their neighbors, a good chere to some.

Good bread and good drinke, a good fier in the hall,
brawne, pudding, and souse, and good mustarde withal.
Biefe, mutton, and Porke, and good Pies of the best,
pig, veale, goose and capon, and turkey wel drest,
Chese, apples, and nuttes, and good Caroles to heare,
as then, in the cuntrey is counted good cheare.

What cost to good husband, is any of this?
good householde provision onely it is:
Of other the like, I do leave out a meny,
that costeth the husband never a peny.

NOTES

[1] Bennett, *op. cit.*, p. 2.

[2] Powers, *op. cit.*, p. 46.

[3] *Ibid.*

[4] *Paston Letters, loc cit.*

[5] Bennett, *op. cit.*, p. 53.

[6] *Ibid.*, p. 54.

[7] Kendall, *Yorkist Age*, pp. 332-338.

[8] Powers, *op. cit.*, p. 43.

[9] *Ibid.*

[10] Ide, *op. cit.*, p. 69.

[11] *Paston Letters, op. cit.*

[12] Ross, *op. cit.*, p. 3.

[13] Kendall, *Richard III*, pp. 155-156.

[14] Powers, *op. cit.*, p. 56.

[15] 1419 London statute, quoted in *Not In God's Image*, pp. 146-147.

[16] Powers, *op. cit.*, pp. 61-62.

[17] Rarely, if ever, did a woman become a physician with a degree from a university. However, women could be come barber-surgeons, a somewhat lesser calling. This requred some years of apprenticeship rather than a course of academic study. See *Not In God's Image*, p. 166.

[18] Quoted in Powers, *op. cit.*, p. 60.

[19] Kendall, *Yorkist Age*, p. 332.

[20] Hartley, *op. cit.*, p. 35.

[21] *Ibid.*, p. 85.

[22] Villages still contained a commons or common land during the Yorkist period. The enclosing of these common grazing lands began during the reigns of the Tudor monarchs and left the peasants with no place to grace their animals.

[23] See Hartley. Her entire book deals with the daily life of the peasant during the latter part of the Middle Ages, and into the Tudor period. It is an excellent and interesting reading resource.

[24] See *The Book of Margery Kempe* for the story of one Yorkist woman who tried, and failed, at many different bye industries.

[25] Hartley, *op. cit.*, p. 261.

[26] Rowland Parker, *The Common Stream: Portrait of An English Village Through 2,000 Years* (New York: Holt, Rinehart & Winston, 1975), pp. 128-129.

[27] *Ibid.*

[28] Hartley, *op. cit.*, pp. 275-276; originally printed in Thomas Tusser's *Five Hundred Points of Husbandry* (London, 1557).

[29] *Ibid.*, p. 256. The poem, again, is from Tusser.

This early woodcut shows a typical occurance in the daily life of the medieval peasant: wild animals damaging the peasant's crops while the peasant, forbidden by law from hunting them, was forced to drive them away with clubs, and build fences against them. Note the peasant woman on the left-side foreground who spun while she tended the evening meal of a root-crop soup (meat was seldom added inasmuch as most meat generally was consumed by the nobility). To the right of the working woman we see medieval men drinking and conversing, while the old man in the center makes fence posts for the youth to construct as a barrier against the wild animals. [Deutsche Fotothek, Dresden.]

CHAPTER FOUR

Women in the Wars of the Roses

The Yorkist Age was a time of determined, independent women. Because of the civil war, women took on roles usually left to men: to defend castles, lead armies, and direct both civil and military policy. Though they were not usually trained in the arts of government or warfare, many women during this period did a creditable job at both when the need arose.

Generally, women became involved in politics only when they felt it necessary to protect the interests of their family. Loyalty to one's family was the primary societal bond during the Yorkist Age, and women especially perceived this. As has been previously discussed, women generally married to further their family's interests; therefore, it is not surprising that family was more important to most Yorkist women than political persuasion or ideology.

In Yorkist society, land represented wealth. Many nobles used the excuse provided by the civil war to try and attain more land militarily by "conquering" the manors belonging to neighboring lords of different political persuasions. To prevent this, men who left their holdings to fight, or merely to visit their other manors, left their wives to defend their property. Margaret Paston, while yet a young woman in her twenties, directed the defense of her husband's Gresham manor against an army which outnumbered her garrison by at least ten to one and led by Lord Molynes. When the manor was finally over-run, Margaret refused to surrender and had to be bodily carried out. She immediately took up residence in a manor nearby and began plotting to get Gresham back into her family's hands.

A similar incident happened to Alice Knyvet. Her husband had left her in charge of Bokenham castle while he attended to business elsewhere. When ordered to give up the castle to the king's troops, Lady Alice replied:[1]

> I will not leave possession of this castle to die therefore; and if you begin to break the peace or make war to get the place of me, I shall defend me. For rather had I in such wise to die that to be slain when my husband cometh home, for he charged me to keep it.

Few women were called upon to defend their lands, but the majority of women during the Yorkist Age did attempt to influence their husbands' political persuasions if they felt that by doing so they could benefit their family. Catherine, Duchess of Buckingham, almost certainly influenced her husband to shift his allegiance from the House of York to the House of Lancaster. Catherine married the Duke of Buckingham soon after her sister, Elizabeth Woodville, became queen. By the time Edward IV died in 1483, the Duke and Duchess had probably achieved an amiable relationship, as was typical in most arranged marriages. After Edward's death, Buckingham supported his cousin, Richard of Gloucester, in his bid for the throne. He may even have fancied himself as the power behind the throne. He was certainly the confidant of the king and had received considerable lands and titles for his support. Yet, suddenly in 1483, the Duke led a revolt against Richard in favor of Henry Tudor. Historians have often wondered why he did this. It is possible that he was persuaded to shift allegiance by his wife, whose loyalty was not to Richard III, or even to Henry Tudor, but to her sister and her sister's children. Elizabeth Woodville stood to gain more with Henry on the throne, than with Richard, for Henry had promised to marry her eldest daughter and make her his queen.[2]

Promoting the interests of her family remained paramount for Margaret of York even after her marriage to Charles, Duke of Burgundy. Her marriage, like so many others of this period, was the result of a treaty between the House of York, and the Duchy of Burgundy. Throughout her marriage, Margaret insured that her husband, who had formerly supported the House of Lancaster, remained loyal to the House of York. Her court became a safe haven for Yorkists who found it necessary to flee England. In 1470, she gave refuge to her brothers, Edward and Richard, when they fled following the revolt of the Earl of Warwick, and she loaned them men and ships to return to England and reclaim the throne. That same year, she acted as mediator between her two brothers Edward and George, Duke of Clarence.[3] She helped to bring about a reconciliation between them but was ultimately unable to save George when, in 1478, he was convicted of treason and executed. After the accession of the Tudor, Henry VII, Margaret continued to give aid to the remaining members of the House of York. In 1485, she supported an uprising led against Henry VII, by her nephew, John de la Pole, Earl of Lincoln. Nearly ten years later she acknowledged that the youth commonly known as Perkin Warbeck was her nephew, Richard, Duke of York (Richard IV) and thus gave credence to the rebellion he led.[4] Her verification of his identity convinced other countries, especially Ireland and Scotland, to recognize him as the son of Edward IV. Unfortunately, this rebellion also failed and the youth was executed in 1499. The Tudor Dynasty remained secure upon the English throne. But Margaret had done her best and probably died with the assurance that she could have done no better for her family.

Some ladies of the Yorkist Age gave up a life of peaceful security to actively support their husband's political aspirations. Such a lady was Cecily Neville, Duchess of York, and mother of Edward IV and Richard III. Married in 1438, by her father Ralph, Earl of Westmorland, to Richard, Duke of York, she devoted the rest of her life to promoting his interests and the interests of their children. She preferred to follow her husband as he traveled throughout Europe on royal business, rather than remain in the comforts of her manors and castles in England. Even pregnancy did not deter her; three of her children were born in France, one in Ireland, and the remainder were born in various castles in England. She supported her husband when he made his bid for the regency of England in 1454, and thus began his long struggle against Queen Margaret over who should rule England on behalf of the mentally incompetent king Henry VI. Duke Richard's battles with the Queen caused Cecily great hardship as she fled from castle to castle with her youngest children, sometimes missing Margaret's advancing army by only hours. In October, 1459, the Yorkist leaders were surprised by Margaret's troops at Ludlow castle in Wales. The Duke and his two older sons fled for their lives; Cecily remained behind with the younger children. When the troops entered the town they found Cecily standing with her children at the market cross. They were immediately taken into custody and sent to the care of Cecily's Lancastrian sister, the Duchess of Buckingham. Cecily remained under the watchful eye of her sister for nearly a year; then when her husband returned in triumph she hurriedly left to greet him. She saw little more of her valiant husband, however, for on December 30, 1460, he and his seventeen year old son, Edmund was killed while fighting Margaret's troops near Wakefield. The death of her husband caused Cecily great grief; she took a vow of chastity and lived the remainder of her life in quiet seclusion at her castle at Berkhamsted, or at her London townhouse of Baynard's castle. She continued to influence her sons Edward, George, and Richard. She disapproved violently of Edward's marriage to Elizabeth Woodville.[5] In 1470, she secretly worked to reunite Edward with his traitorous brother, George. When

Edward died in 1483, she apparently supported her youngest son Richard's usurpation of his nephew's throne, perhaps feeling, as did many other people at the time, that it was better for the realm to be ruled by an adult than by a child.[6] Cecily outlived her husband and all four of her sons, but when she died she may have had some satisfaction in seeing her granddaughter on the throne of England and knowing that her great-grandson would in time inherit that throne.[7]

Three great women stand out during the Yorkist Age for the active role they played in the civil war between the Houses of York and Lancaster. It is possible that, but for the influence these women had on England's policies, the so-called Wars of the Roses might never have begun and they certainly would have ended sooner than they did and with less bloodshed.

Margaret of Anjou married King Henry VI of England in 1455, to seal a treaty of peace between England and France. When she arrived in England, a girl of fifteen, she found in Henry a weak man and a weaker king over whom various factions battled for influence.[8] Margaret refused to remain above these political rivalries; she threw her influence to the party led by the king's uncle, Cardinal Beaufort.[9]

As she grew older, Margaret herself began to take an active role in governing the country. She began by administering her own estates and went on to declare herself regent for her husband when his periodic fits of madness made him incapable of ruling. A contemporary remarks that she was "a great and intensely active woman for she spares no pains to pursue her business towards an end and conclusion favourable to her power."[10] Her high-handed ways offended many members of the nobility, especially the Duke of York who was heir to the throne until Margaret should have a child. Margaret feared the Duke and attempted to keep him from having any power over the king. The Duke sought what he felt was his rightful place in the council which governed the country. Thus, in the power struggle between Margaret and the Duke of York began the "Wars of the Roses."

Matters came to a head in August of 1453, when Henry completely lost touch with reality; recognizing no one, he lapsed into a world of his own. On October 13, Margaret gave birth to an heir whom she named Edward.[11] After the birth of her child, she petitioned Parliament to name her as sole regent for her husband. Parliament refused this request, preferring instead to name the Duke of York as regent. Margaret found herself temporarily without power, relegated to the background of events. However, in January of 1455, the King recovered and Margaret and her party reassumed control of the government. Margaret herself obtained control of the privy seal and used it to appoint her supporters to office. At this point she hesitated to openly break with York, since she was not yet ready to risk an open battle with him. Yet, between 1455 and 1459, York's influence at court and in the government was steadily diminished. By the summer of 1459, two armed camps had developed in England. In September these two camps met on the battlefield. We do not know much about the Battle of Blore Heath, except that it was won by Richard Neville, Earl of Salisbury, and that Queen Margaret was forced to flee. But the Yorkist victory was short-lived, for in October, Margaret surprised York near his home of Ludlow Castle, forcing the Duke and his oldest sons to flee to Ireland in fear of their lives. For awhile Margaret was again the undisputed ruler of England.

Five months later, the Duke of York returned to England at the head of an army. On July 2, 1460, he entered London. At the same time, Margaret fled the city with her infant son. She sought refuge at Coventry, while her generals, accompanied by King Henry, marched to challenge York. At Northampton, about a days march from London, the armies of York and Lancaster met again. King Henry's forces were defeated, and the monarch captured and placed in confinement in the Tower of London. The Yorkists, victorious at last, sent messages out from London calling for a sitting of Parliament for October, 1460. There the Duke of York demanded that Parliament declare King Henry incompetent to rule and consequently crown him king. Parliament refused, but offered a compromise: York would rule as Henry's regent until the King died, and then York himself would become King. This arrangement disinherited the young son of Henry and Margaret, and Margaret refused to accept it. She fled to Wales, taking the child with her. Enroute she was ambushed and lost her jewels and other valuables, but she and her son, penniless as they were, were able to make it safely to refuge with their supporters at Herlech. There she cautiously set about raising another army.

Three months later, Margaret's army faced the Duke of York on the snowy ground outside of Sandal Castle near Wakefield. York's forces were badly outnumbered and never had a chance to win the battle. The Duke of York, his seventeen year old son Edmund, and his brother-in-law, the Earl of Salisbury, were all killed in the fighting. Margaret, who could be very vicious when she chose to, had the bodies beheaded and the heads placed above the gates of York. The Duke's head she had crowned with a wreath of paper and straw.

Immediately following the battle of Wakefield, Margaret began to march towards London. With her traveled an army composed mostly of Scot mercaneries. The English people, the majority of whom had supported Henry as the rightful ruler of England, were horrified at the idea of bringing an army of Scots into England. Most English saw the Scots, who were their traditional enemies, as being at least half-barbarian, uncivilized troops who would rape and plunder their way throughout the countryside. Actually, Margaret's army probably did no more raping and plunering than did the armies of the Duke of York, or the Earl of Warwick. Nevertheless, by her action of hiring a foreign army to enter England and fight against Englishmen, Margaret lost a great deal of support among the English people.[12]

On February 17, 1460, Margaret's army met the army of the Earl of Warwick at St. Albans. Here Margaret won a major victory and was able to free her husband, King Henry, who traveled with Warwick. After her victory, Margaret attempted to enter London, but the evil reputation of her Scots troops preceeded her and the Londoners shut the city gates. Margaret was forced to retreat, and on February 26, Edward, the eighteen year old Duke of York, entered London amidst much acclamation and rejoicing. A few days later he was crowned King Edward IV.

Margaret retreated north of the Trent and attempted to regain her throne. She still commanded the loyalty of most of the English nobility; Edward was popular mainly in the south and around London. On March 29, Margaret faced Edward's troops at Towton, near York. Here the two armies met and fought "one of the bloodiest battles ever fought on English soil."[13] Some 28,000 men died at Towton, including five peers (Northumberland, Clifford, Neville, Dacre, and Wells). When the battle was over the Lancastrian army had been completely routed. Margaret, with her husband and son, fled to Scotland.

In Scotland, Margaret offered the Scots king, James III, the English city of Berwick if he would supply her with troops. Later in the year she traveled to France and offered the French king, Louis XI, the English port of Calais if he would supply her with troops. Neither monarch was very generous to her. A few French mercaneries accompanied her back to Scotland. A Scots army crossed the border in July, 1463, and beseiged Norham Castle. But their efforts failed, and the Scots returned home.

Margaret began to frantically seek other alliances. She turned first to Philip of Burgundy, who gave her some money but refused to supply her with troops. She turned again to the French king, but on October 8, he signed a truce with Edward IV, recognizing him as the lawful king of England. Soon after the Anglo-French truce was signed, the Scots also began to negotiate a truce with Edward. Suddenly, the Lancastrian refugees found themselves totally without support. Finally, in July, 1465, Henry VI was captured and imprisoned in the Tower. Margaret and her son, their cause temporarily lost, fled to her home of Anjou.

Margaret spent the next five years in the general poverty of her father's court. In 1470, Margaret received an unexpected summons from the French king. He wished her to meet with Richard Neville, the Earl of Warwick, who was volunteering to return her to her throne. Margaret scornfully refused to meet with him. He had faithfully supported the Yorkist usurpation of the English throne, and had been responsible for the rumors which branded her son a bastard, the son of the Duke of Somerset rather than of Henry VI. But, as Louis reminded Margaret, no one else was anxious to champion her cause. Margaret agreed, and on July 22, 1470, she met with Warwick at Angers in France. Margaret kept the haughty Earl on his knees for fifteen minutes before she would accept his apology for past wrongs. Then the two sat together to plan their strategy. Warwick agreed to raise an army, return to England, and return Henry VI to the throne. Margaret agreed to betrothe her seventeen year old son, Edward, to Warwick's fifteen year old daughter, Anne. However, the marriage would be delayed until Henry was safely back on the throne. Warwick agreed, and on September 9, after several months of careful preparation, set sail for England. The Queen, her son, Warwick's wife and daughter remained in France.

Warwick caught Edward IV unprepared. On September 30, surrounded by two hostile armies, the King and his youngest brother fled to Burgundy. Warwick marched unimpeded into London, and freed Henry VI from the Tower. Margaret, however, still did not fully trust Warwick, and so she delayed her departure from France for several months. Finally, in March, she was assured of the safety of the trip. But she had waited too long. On March 2, 1471, Edward, with an army which he had raised in Burgundy, sailed for England. On April 14, Easter Sunday, Edward's army faced the forces led by the Earl of Warwick at Barnet. When the battle was over, one thousand men lay dead, including the Earl of Warwick. This news greeted Margaret when she stepped ashore on English soil later that same day. Margaret immediately wanted to return to the safety of France, but her old friend, the Duke of Somerset, and possibly also her son who was fighting for his birthright, persuaded her to remain.[14]

Margaret reluctantly agreed to stay in England, but she refused to face Edward with the small army that she had brought from France. Quickly and secretly, hoping that Edward would not learn of her movements, she began to march towards Wales where Jaspar Tudor awaited her. Unfortunately, it is difficult to move an army across country unnoticed and Edward had reliable informers. He knew that Margaret had landed, and guessed where she would try to go. He rushed his army north, hoping to cut her off before she reached Wales and reinforcements. Margaret knew that she would lose any confrontation with Edward and desperately tried to stay ahead of him. It became a race to the Severn River. If they could cross into Wales, Margaret's army, and her son, would be safe. By Friday, May 3, it looked as if they would succeed. Early that morning they approached the city of Gloucester. Here they hoped to rest and provision themselves, secure behind the massive castle walls. But the governor of the castle was loyal to his lord, the brother of Edward IV. He refused to open the gates to Margaret's army. There was nothing they could do but keep marching, hoping to reach the Severn before Edward caught up with them. But Margaret's luck had run out. By four that afternoon, she reached the river but Edward was too close to allow the entire army to cross safely. So, although the army had marched fifty miles over rough terrain in the past thirty-six hours and everyone was exhausted, hungry, and thirsty, they had no choice but to turn and prepare for battle.

The Battle of Tewkesbury, fought on Saturday, May 4, 1471, was a disaster for Margaret. Her troops were completely routed by Edward. Many of her staunchest supporters were killed or captured. And most important, Edward of Lancaster, the seventeen year old prince upon whom all his mother's hopes were pinned, was killed while engaged in his first battle.[15]

Margaret did not learn of her son's death until the next day. She and her ladies, who had taken refuge in a house of religion some distance from the battlefield, were captured, and Margaret was brutally informed by Sir William Stanley that her son was dead. The news sent Margaret into shock. From this shock she never totally recovered. Ultimately Edward IV had her returned to France to live the remainder of her days in poverty. Her grandiose schemes had failed, yet she had been a gallant woman who had fought for what she perceived to be the rights of her husband and son.

Margaret was supplanted as queen by Elizabeth Woodville, the daughter of Richard, Lord Rivers, and his wife Jacquetta, Dowager Duchess of Bedford. Elizabeth's first marriage was to Sir John Grey who died while fighting for the Lancastrian cause at the Battle of St. Albans in 1461. After his death, his widow and two young sons were left impoverished, causing Elizabeth to return to her parent's home. It is not known how Elizabeth met King Edward, but legend says she confronted him in the royal forest to petition that her deceased husband's property be returned to her sons. Edward not only ordered the lands returned, but on May 1, 1464, secretly married the Lady Elizabeth. Later, above the objections of his family and most of the nobility—who were scandalized that a King of England would marry a poor widow—Edward made her his queen.

Elizabeth used her good fortune to help her family. She secured advantageous marriages for her five brothers and seven sisters, and secured government posts for her father and brothers. Unfortunately, by preferring her own family, Elizabeth earned the enmity of the established nobility who felt that such preferments should go to them. She also managed to drive a wedge between her relatives and Edward's family. This wedge had been driven so deeply, that when Edward died both sides felt that they had to protect themselves from the other.[16]

As Queen, Elizabeth found herself in a position for which she was unprepared. Because of her lack of preparation to be a queen, and act as a queen, Elizabeth often used her new power unwisely. In 1468, Sir Thomas Cook, former Lord Mayor of London, refused to sell a tapestry worth £800 to Elizabeth's mother, Lady Jacquetta. Some time later, Sir Thomas was accused of treason (a charge on which he was later acquitted). During the time he spent in prison, Elizabeth had his house ransacked and the tapestry taken. Sir Thomas never recovered it.[17] His loss inspired enormous enmity between the two--a bitterness which filtered down to others who feared similar treatment.

In 1467, Elizabeth conspired to have the Earl of Desmond and his two sons executed because he had once said to King Edward, in a moment of confidence, that he thought the king would have done better for the realm if he had married a foreign princess.[18] Events such as this, coupled with the fact that she was emotionally cold and uncaring about people outside her immediate family, made Queen Elizabeth very unpopular with the English people.

Elizabeth became a prime mover in the events which occured following the death of Edward IV. Edward died suddenly,[19] leaving his twelve year old son, Edward V, as heir to the realm. The king's will stipulated that a council comprised of several of Elizabeth's relatives and Edward's close friends, and headed by Edward's brother, Richard, Duke of Gloucester, should rule the realm while the young king was in his minority. Elizabeth, herself, was not to be a member of this council.

During the years following her marriage, Elizabeth had managed to alienate Richard of Gloucester. Mancini relates that Richard blamed her for the execution of his brother, George.[20] And, although the king was directly responsible for George's execution, it is possible that Elizabeth was covertly urging her husband to have George dispatched. A theory, held by some historians,[21] states that George, somehow, had learned that the marriage between Elizabeth and Edward was irregular, and that it might be invalid. Both the king and queen had reason to believe, considering George's background, that he would use this information for his personal advancement. This would occur if Edward's children were declared bastards, for once their legitimacy was thrown out, George would automatically become king upon Edward's death, since he was the next heir to the throne- provided, of course, that if such a situation occured, Edward did not marry again and have children by his new wife. But this is mere speculation; all we do know is that George was executed for a relatively light offense—usurping the king's justice; that this must be considered a minor infraction can be taken from his previous record and the king's attitudes towards that record, for Edward had forgiven George five years earlier of a much greater treason: he had rebelled against the king! It is also acknowledged that Edward *wanted* his brother dead, for he acted as prosecutor at George's trial, ignoring the pleas of his mother, his brother Richard, and his sisters to spare George's life.[22] If it is true that Edward's marriage was invalid and that George knew it, it would explain Edward's insistence upon his brother's death and especially upon George's private and unpublicized execution within the Tower. And it would help explain Richard III's subsequent attitude toward his sister-in-law, for Richard was certainly aware that she had wanted his brother dead, but being unaware of the real reason, put it down to personal spite and ambition. This theory also explains why Elizabeth feared Richard, for she couldn't chance that he, too, find out that her marriage to Edward IV was invalid.

Elizabeth's first move, then, after her husband's death, was to neglect to inform Richard of what had happened. Next, she persuaded the council to have her son brought quickly and secretly from his castle of Ludlow in Wales. She hoped to have him crowned, and a council of regency set up—possibly with her at its head—before Richard could learn what had happened. Unfortunately for Elizabeth, Richard learned of the scheme, met the royal party outside London, arrested the young king's guardians (Anthony, Lord Rivers, the Queen's brother, and her son by her first marriage, Richard), and took charge of the young king. Elizabeth, in a panic, fled into Westminster sanctuary with her youngest son and her daughters.

Edward IV's widow continued to plot from within the sanctuary. In June, she conspired with Lord Hastings, Lord Stanley, and Bishop Morton, to overthrow, and possibly murder, Richard of Gloucester. Richard learned of the plot from a retainer in the service of Lord Hastings, and had Hastings executed, and Stanley and Morton put under house arrest. On June 16, Elizabeth agreed to let her youngest son leave sanctuary to be with his brother. Whether she did this voluntarily, or under threat of violence is unknown.

In July, the story was made public that Edward IV had not been validly married to Elizabeth. The official account declared that before Edward IV had met Elizabeth he had precontracted himself to the Lady Eleanor Butler. That relationship had not been annuled when Edward married Elizabeth. The result was that Edward had been involved in a bigamous relationship, and that his children by Elizabeth were illigetimate. Based on that information, Richard of Gloucester ascended the throne of England and was crowned King as Richard III.[24]

Elizabeth refused to accept that none of her children would sit upon the English throne. In October, 1483, although still confined to sanctuary, Elizabeth encouraged the Duke of Buckingham's rebellion against Richard. Originally, the goal of the rebellion had been to put the sons of Edward IV on the throne, but in September, rumors began to spread throughout the country that the children had been murdered by Richard III.[25] Since the young princes had not been seen in several months, and since Richard did not produce them to disprove the rumors, most people involved in the rebellion accepted the rumors as true and switched their allegiance to Henry Tudor, the Lancastrian claimant to the throne of England.

Buckingham's rebellion failed, but Elizabeth continued to plot against Richard. Communicating with Margaret Beaufort, Henry Tudor's mother, Elizabeth informed the Dowager Duchess that she would not be adverse to a betrothal between Margaret's son and her own daughter, the princess Elizabeth. Margaret accepted, and the royal betrothal took place on Christmas Day, 1483.

In spite of the betrothal, little changed. As the months dragged on, it became apparent to Elizabeth that Richard was going to remain king—at least for a while.

Buckingham's rebellion had failed, and the country was at peace. People were beginning to accept Richard as their king. And Richard wanted his nieces out of sanctuary, which would lend his rule an air of conciliation and earnestness for peace both at home, and abroad. On March 1, 1484, Elizabeth made a deal with Richard III. Her daughters would leave sanctuary if they would be acknowledged and protected at the king's court. Richard would see to their honorable marriages, and provide each with a dowry. Richard, at the same time, promised Elizabeth some dower property and a yearly stipend—although she would not receive the title of Queen Dowager.[26] It is not known whether or not Elizabeth actually left sanctuary when her daughters did. Certainly she seems to have reconciled herself to Richard's rule, for soon after her release from sanctuary she wrote to her eldest son, Thomas, who was in exile with Henry Tudor, that he could safely return home to England.

By Christmas, 1484, the political situation had changed—one more time. In April, Richard's only son had died unexpectedly.[27] Eight months later it was obvious to everyone that Richard's queen was mortally ill. Rumors began to spread through the court that when Queen Anne died, Richard would marry his niece, Elizabeth. It is not known whether or not Elizabeth's mother had anything to do with the circulation of these rumors. Certainly a marriage between an uncle and a niece was not impossible during the Middle Ages. A dispensation from Rome was obtainable, although it might be difficult.

It is possible that Elizabeth, Edward's widow, may have seen her daughter's marriage to Richard III as a way to make her daughter Queen of England--and thus increase her own importance and position in the realm. But, it is equally possible that she was disgusted by the rumors that linked her daughter with the man who had disinherited her sons by Edward IV.[28]

After the defeat and death of Richard in August, 1485, the new king, Henry VII (1457-1509), was reminded of his betrothal to the princess Elizabeth. After he married Elizabeth, he restored to her mother her title as Queen Dowager and some of the revenues that went with the position, all of which she had been deprived of during Richard III's brief reign.[30] But Queen Dowager Elizabeth's good fortune did not last long. In 1487, the remaining Yorkist sympathizers revolted against the Tudor king. At the same time, Henry stripped Elizabeth of her title and revenues, and ordered her removed to Bermondsey Abbey. The official reason given for this action was that she had endangered Henry and his cause when, in 1484, she allowed her daughters to leave sanctuary and take up residence at Richard's court. The real reason, many historians have argued, is that Elizabeth somehow involved herself in the Yorkist revolt. Why she would do so, when her daughter was queen and her grandson would someday be king, remains a mystery. Some historians have suggested that Elizabeth loved intrigue and had little common sense, but this seems to slander a woman who sometimes made disasterous decisions, but whose actions were usually motivated by her psychological need to protect and advance her family. Other historians have suggested that she learned that Henry VII and the Lancastrian party, rather than Richard III, had caused the deaths of her two sons. Or, perhaps, her sons, or at least one of them, were not dead and this rebellion was a smokescreen behind which the real rebellion, one to put one of the sons of Edward IV on the throne, was hidden. Whatever the reason, Elizabeth was in royal disfavor and remained so until her death in 1492.[31]

Margaret Beaufort had better luck than did either Margaret of Anjou or Elizabeth Woodville in placing her son on the throne. Margaret, herself a descendent of Edward III (1312 - 1377; reigned 1327 - 1377),[32] married

Edmund Tudor, the son of Owen Tudor and Queen Catherine of Valois, when she was thirteen. The marriage was apparently a happy one, for legend says that Margaret chose the handsome young earl as her husband.[33] Unfortunately, in November of 1456, Edmund died, possibly as a result of wounds received while fighting in Wales. Three months later, on January 28, 1457, Margaret gave birth to a son whom she named Henry, possibly in honor of his uncle, the king.

Margaret lived peacefully at Richmond for several years under the guardianship of Edmond's brother, Jaspar, Earl of Pembroke. But the civil war disrupted their peaceful lives. Jaspar fought for his half-brother, Henry VI. After the battle of Mortimer's Cross, he was forced to flee and Margaret and her son surrendered themselves to William, Lord Herbert. Lord Herbert received the wardship of young Henry from Edward IV, and he raised the youth among his own children.[34] Margaret remarried in 1464, accepting Henry Stafford as her second husband, and during the years 1464 - 1471, she probably saw her son only on rare occasions. In 1471, Jaspar Tudor and his fourteen year old nephew took part in the Lancastrian revolt which briefly returned Henry VI to the throne. But when the revolt ultimately failed, and Henry VI and his son were dead, Jaspar was forced to flee again. This time he took his nephew with him, for the youth, descended from Edward III through his mother and from the royal house of France through his father, could now be considered a serious contender for the English throne.

Margaret, left behind, seemed to reconcile herself to the Yorkist rulers and married her third husband, Thomas, Lord Stanley, a supporter of Edward IV. Secretly, however, Margaret continued to communicate with her son.

When Edward IV died in 1483, Margaret began to actively work for the restoration of Lancastrian rule. She used her physician, Dr. Lewis, as a liason between herself and Edward IV's widow, Queen Elizabeth who had sought sanctuary at Westminster.[35]   Margaret was able to persuade the Queen that her only hope of seeing one of her children on the English throne was to betrothe one of her daughters to her son, Henry Tudor. A union between a daughter of Edward IV and the only Lancastrian claimant who could trace his lineage back to Edward III would surely unite England and bring to the English peace and prosperity! Elizabeth agreed. But the revolt of 1483, ended in failure. Henry refused to land in England and lead the revolt. Instead he returned to the safety of Brittany.

Margaret's role in the rebellion did not go unnoticed. Her estates were confiscated, and her husband was told to keep her under constant surveillance. This was a mistake on Richard III's part, for during the next year Margaret persuaded her husband that his best interests lay in supporting her son. In 1485, when Henry invaded England, Lord Stanley turned traitor to Richard III on the battlefield at Market Bosworth, thus causing Richard's defeat and death.

Henry VII openly acknowledged that he owed his throne largely to the work his mother had done in England to help him. He honored her by allowing her to sign herself "Margaret R" and she was treated as a Queen Dowager. At Henry's request, his first parliament gave Margaret the rights and privileges of a "sole person, not a wyfe ne covert of any husband. . . ." and she was to have sole authority over her property and her life. In short, she was to be treated as a man—not as a woman dependent upon her husband. This was an almost unheard of honor for any woman during this period of time.

Once Margaret had achieved her goal of having her son crowned King of England, she retired from public life, and lived quietly in seclusion, coming to court only for rare family occasions. However, throughout the remainder of her life she corresponded regularly with her son, giving him advice. When she died in 1509, she was a well respected and loved woman throughout England.

The period of the Wars of the Roses was a time of great freedom for women. Henry Tudor, perhaps, saw that there was some danger in this, for during his reign, and later, during the reign of his son, Henry VIII (1491-1547), women were once more confined to the single role of wife and mother. During their reigns we do not see powerful, aggressive queens and noblewomen directing their own affairs and the affairs of the country. It is not until the reigns of Mary (1516 - 1558; reigned, 1553 - 1558), and Elizabeth Tudor (Elizabeth I, 1533 - 1603; reigned 1558 - 1603), both great-granddaughters of Margaret Beaufort and Elizabeth Woodville, that women again have the power to direct the English nation.

NOTES

[1] Quotation in Kendall, *Yorkist Age*, p. 414.

[2] This may assume that the young princes were either dead or that everyone assumed that they were dead. Otherwise, it would surely be fatal for them if Henry Tudor came to the throne and married their sister, for to do so he would have to reverse the bill *Titulus Regius* which made the children of Edward IV bastards. This, of course, would make Elizabeth's brothers the rightful heirs to the throne, and thus, at the same time, negate his own right to the English crown. It is also possible, of course, that the boys were alive and that Elizabeth hoped to foment a new civil war, figuring that during the chaos that would follow a war between Henry Tudor and King Richard III, the Woodvilles could regain their power.

[3] George had aligned himself with Warwick and the Lancastrian party against his brother in the hopes that he would eventually be made king. When the revolt failed, George was more than eager to have his brother forgive him.

[4] History is unsure exactly who Perkin Warbeck really was. A few historians believe that he may actually have been Richard IV (see, Audrey Williamson, *The Mystery of the Princes: An Investiga-*

tion Into A Supposed Murder. Gairdner, in the appendix to his *Richard III*, agrees with the official version put about by Henry VII, that Warbeck was a Flemish merchant's son who was coached in his role of Richard IV by Margaret of Burgundy. Kendall, in his appendix to *Richard III*, assumes that the princes were murdered during the reign of Richard, either on orders of Richard himself, or by the Duke of Buckingham. He does not mention the mystery of Perkin Warbeck at all).

[5]Mancini, *op. cit.*, pp. 61, 63.

[6]We can suppose Cecily's approval since Richard resided in her house until his coronation.

[7]Elizabeth of York was the granddaughter, Henry VIII the great-grandson.

[8]Henry had bouts of insanity which he may have inherited from his maternal grandfather, King Charles of France.

[9]Cardinal Beaufort was the son of John, Duke of Lancaster and Catherine Swynford. He died in 1447.

[10]John Gillingham, *The Wars of the Roses* (Baton Rouge, LA: Louisiana State University Press, 1981), p. 99. No original source is given.

[11]Since Henry was insane during most of Margaret's pregnancy, and since they had been married for ten years without any children, the legitimacy of the young prince was disputed. It was commonly believed, at least by the Yorkists, that Edward of Lancaster's father was actually the Duke of Somerset.

[12]*Croyland Chronicle*, pp. 422-423. See, also, Ross, *op. cit.*, p. 31; and, Gillingham, *op. cit.*, pp. 122-124.

[13]Gillingham, *ibid.*, p. 134.

[14]For details of both the battles of Barnet and Tewkesbury, see *Historie of the Arrivall of King Edward IV*, ed. J. Bruce (London: Camden Society, 1838). This record gives the official Yorkist interpretation of the events of those precarious and trying months.

[15]It is a later Tudor legend that young Edward was killed after the battle. All contemporary sources (*i.e.*, the *Arrivall*, Warkworth's *Chronicle*, and the *Croyland Chronicle*) state that Edward was killed

in battle.

[16]Mancini, *op. cit.*, pp. 61, 63, 67, 69. See also, Thomas More, *The Historie of King Richard III*, and Kendall, *Richard III*, pp. 189-190.

[17]*Great Chronicle of London*, ed. A. H. Thomas and I. D. Thornley (London: Camden Society, 1938), pp. 204-208; cf. Ross, *op. cit.*, pp. 99-100.

[18]Kendall, *op. cit.*, p. 80.

[19]The chronicles are vague about how Edward died, with speculation ranging from catching cold on a fishing trip (Vergil, *op. cit.*, pp. 171-172), apoplexy (Commynes, *loc. cit.*), physical excess (*Croyland Chronicle*, p. 483). He died on April 9, 1483, after an illness which lasted ten days.

[20]Mancini, *op. cit.*, p. 63.

[21]See especially, Kendall, *op. cit.*, pp. 258-260.

[22]Ross, *op. cit.*, pp. 241-244.

[23]The actual existence of the plot is conjecture. Richard alleged that there was a plot and reacted to forestall it. Historians have debated the issue; see Alison Hanham, "Richard III, Lord Hastings and the Historians," in *English Historical Review* LXXXVIII (1972); Wolfe, "When and Why Did Hastings Lose His Head?" in *English Historical Review* LXXXIX (1974); Alison Hanham, "Hasting Redivivus," in *English Historical Review* XC (1975); and, Wolffe, "Hastings Reinterred," in *English Historical Review* XCI (1976).

[24]For arguments concerning the alleged precontract, see Kendall, *op. cit.*, pp. 256-261, and 555-556; Ross, *op. cit.*, pp. 89-92.

[25]*Croyland Chronicle*, p. 491.

[26]Kendall, *op. cit.*, pp. 344-345.

[27]Edward of Middleham, Richard and Anne's eleven year old son. His death was sudden and unexpected. No cause is known, although some historians have speculated that the youth, like his mother, died of tuberculosis. However, there is no contemporary indication that he was frail, and, the fact that his death was unex-

pected, and that his parents were not with him when he died, seems to indicate that the child died from some sudden illness or accident.

[28]*Croyland Chronicle*, pp. 499-500.

[29]S. B. Chrimes, *Henry VII* (Berkeley, CA: University of California Press, 1972).

[30]Kendall, *op. cit.*, pp. 491-492.

[31]Margaret was a great-granddaughter of Edward III. She was the daughter of John Beaufort, first Duke of Somerset.

[32]E. M. G. Rough, *The Lady Margaret: A Memoir of Lady Margaret Beaufort* (London: Oxford University Press, 1924), p. 20.

[33]Herbert was being rewarded for his support of York. However, he appears to have been honestly fond of young Henry and hoped to arrange a wedding between the youth and his daughter, Maud.

[34]It may have been a coincidence that Dr. Lewis was also the Queen's physician, but more likely he was sent to Elizabeth by Margaret. A physician could enter the sanctuary less noticed than other people and would not be an obvious link between the two women.

[35]Chrimes, *op. cit.*, p. 57.

[36]*Rotuli Parliamentum*, VI.284.

SELECT BIBLIOGRAPHY

Bennett, Henry. *The Pastons and Their England.* Cambridge: The University Press, 1968.

Chrimes, S. B. *Henry VII.* Berkeley: University of California Press, 1975.

Chronicles of the Abbey of Croyland, ed. Henry T. Riley (cited as *Croyland Chronicles*). London: George Bell and Sons, 1908.

Cunnington, Phillis. *Medieval and Tudor Costume.* Boston, MA: Plays, Inc., 1968.

Geis, Francis and Joseph Geis. *Women in the Middle Ages.* New York: Barnes & Noble, 1978.

Gillingham, John. *The Wars of the Roses.* Baton Rouge: Louisiana State University Press, 1981.

Great Chronicle of London, ed. A. H. Thomas and I. D. Thornley (cited as *London Chronicle*). London: Camden Society, 1938.

Hartley, Dorothy. *Lost Country Life.* New York: Pantheon Books, 1979.

Hartley, Dorothy and Margaret Elliot, *Life and Work of People in Medieval England—the Fifteenth Century.* London: G.P. Putnam & Sons, 1926.

Historie of the Arrivall of King Edward IV, ed. J. Bruce. London: Camden Society, 1838.

Ide, Arthur Frederick. *Special Sisters: Woman in the*

European Middle Ages. 4th ed. Mesquite: Ide House, 1983.

Ingulph's Chronicle of the Abbey of Croyland, ed. Henry T. Riley. London: George Bell & Sons, 1908.

Jacob, E. F. *The Fifteenth Century, 1399-1485.* Oxford: Oxford University Press, 1961.

Kendall, Paul Murray. *Richard III.* New York: W. W. Norton & Co., 1955.

————. *The Yorkist Age.* London: Allen & Unwin, 1962.

Lander, J. R. *Crown and Nobility, 1450-1509.* London: Edwin Arnold; Montreal: McGill-Queen's University Press, 1976.

Mancini, Dominic. *The Usurpation of Richard III.* Ed. C. A. J. Armstrong. Oxford: Clarendon Press, 1969.

Not In God's Image, ed. Julia Faolin and Laura Martines. New York: Harper & Row, 1973.

Parker, Rowland. *The Common Stream: Portrait of An English Village Through 2,000 Years.* New York: Holt, Rinehart & Winston, 1975.

Power, Eileen. *Medieval Women.* Cambridge: The University Press, 1975.

Ramsay, J. H. *Lancaster and York.* Oxford: Clarendon Press, 1892.

Ross, Charles. *Edward IV.* Berkeley: University of California Press, 1974.

Ross, Charles. *Richard III*. Berkeley: University of California Press, 1981.

Rough, E. M. G. *The Lady Margaret: A Memoir of Lady Margaret Beaufort*. London: Oxford University Press, 1924.

Saccio, Peter. *Shakespeare's English Kings*. New York: Oxford University Press, 1977.

Scott, A. F. *Every One A Witness: The Plantagenet Age*. New York: Thomas Y. Crowell Co., 1975.

Stenton, Doris Mary. *The English Woman in History* New York: Shocken Books, 1977.

Tudor-Craig, Pamela. *Richard III*. London: Metheun, 1976.

Vergil, Polydore. *Anglica Historia*. London: Camden Society, 1950.

Williamson, Audrey. *The Mystery of the Princes*. Gloucestershire: For the Historical Society, 1978.

INDEX

A
adultery. 36
Agnes, Countess of Dunbar . . 46
Anne Beauchamp 11n, 16
. . . . 17, 37n.
Anne Mortimer . . . . .10n.
Anne Neville. 7, 9, 17, 25
32-34, 38n, 47, 67, 74
Anne of York. 47
annulment 37n
Anthony, Lord Rivers 7, 8
. . . . 19n, 72
Augustine, St. 16

B
Battle of
Barnet. 5, 32, 68, 79n
Blore Heath 64
Bosworth Market. 11n, 24, 25
Mortimer's Cross. 76
St. Alban's .1, 2, 3, 28, 66, 69
Tewkesbury 5, 10n, 32
. . . . 69, 79n
Towton. 66
Wakefield. 2, 65
Beauchamp Pageant 17
Beauchamp, Anne *see*
Anne Beauchamp
Beauchamp, Richard (Earl of
Warwick). 17, 37n
Beaufort, cardinal 63, 79n
Beaufort, duke of Somerset. 2, 3
Beaufort, Joan 22, 29
Beaufort, Margaret. 16, 34
. . . . 73, 78
Berwick (city). 66
birth control. 53
Blanche, duchess of
Lancaster 29
Boccaccio 16
Boleyn, Anne . . . . .38n.
Bona of Savoy 3
bourgoisie, rise of 6, 48-54

Bridgit of York 16
Butler, Eleanor 9, 73
bye industries. 50-51

C
Calais (city-port). 66
Canon Law. 35
Caxton, William 17, 19n
Calley, Richard. 30, 32, 33
Catherine of Valois 30, 76
Catherine, duchess of
Buckingham. 60
Cecily of York 11n, 16, 22
. . . . 47, 61, 62, 79n
Charles of Burgundy . .3, 23, 61
Charles, dauphin of
France. 11, 24
chastity 62
Chaucer, William 16, 19n
childbearing 53-54
children. . . 13-17, 34-35, 54-55
discipline of 15
education of. 13-17
City of God 16
Clare, Elizabeth. 47
cloth industry. 43-44
clothing, fashion . . 43-44, 51-52
Cook, Sir Thomas 70
Council of Regency 8
of the North. 7
of Wales. 7
Croyland Chronicles. 2, 32

D
de la Pole, John (Earl of
Lincoln) 24, 37n, 61
de Pisan, Catherine 45-46
de Vere, John (Earl of
Oxford). 3, 11n
divorce 34
dowry. 22
Duchy of Burgundy. 3

Names of women discussed are in **bold type face.**

E

education. 13, 20
Edmund (son of
   Edward III) 10n
Edward of York 47, 62, 65
Edward I 46
Edward III 10, 12n, 46
  . . . . 75, 77
Edward IV 1, 2, 3, 4, 6, 8
  . . . . 9, 10, 10n, 11n, 16, 17
  . . . 21, 22-24, 28-29, 32, 36
  . . . . . 47, 49, 51, 60, 61, 66
  . . . .67-71, 72-73, 74, 76-77
  . . . . .81n
  death of. 8
  marriage of. 3, 4, 9, 28
  . . . . 29, 70
  marriage, problem of 3
  . . . . . . 4, 70-71, 73, 79n
  trade policies of 6
Edward V 8, 12n, 71
Edward of Lancaster 67-69
Edward of York 9
Elizabeth I (Tudor) 78
Elizabeth, duchess of
Suffolk 37n
Elizabeth Woodville
  (*nee* Grey, queen of
  Edward IV) 3, 4, 8-9
  . . . . 16, 19n, 23, 25
  . . . . .28-29, 60, 62
  . . . . 69-71, 78
  feelings towards
    Richard III. 8, 73-74
Elizabeth Woodville
  (princess, daughter of
  Edward IV) . . .10, 24-25, 74

F

Ferrars, Elizabeth 28
festivals. 54-55

G

gentry 21-22, 26, 41-48
George, duke of Clarence
  . . . . 4, 7, 23-24, 32-33, 37n
  . . . . . 41, 47, 61, 71-72, 78

George, duke of Clarence
  death of. 7, 11n, 61, 71
  treason of 7, 37n, 61
 71-72
Grey, Sir John 28, 69
  see also Elizabeth Woodville
  (queen of Edward IV)
Grey, Richard. 8
guilds 50
gynophobia 50

H

Henry IV 22, 23
Henry V 10n, 30
Henry VI 1, 2, 5, 6, 9, 10
  . . . . 27, 29, 37n, 62, 63, 64
  . . . . .67, 74, 75
Henry VII 9, 10, 24, 25
  . . . . .34, 38n, 60
Henry VIII. 78, 79n
Howard, John. 36n
Humphrey, duke of
  Gloucester 12n

I

Ide, Arthur Frederick. 46
Isabel of Clarence . . 11, 23, 37n
interiors, design &
  decoration 44-45, 51, 54
Italian Relation. 14

J

Jacquetta, duchess of
Bedord 29, 30, 69, 70
James I (king of Scots) 29
James III (king of Scots). . . .66
John, duke of Lancaster
  (son of Edward III) 10
  . . . . .22, 29, 79n
John, duke of Bedford 30
John, duke of York 47

K

Kendall, Paul Murray 51
Kynvet, Alice 46, 59-60

L

Langton, Agnes. 49
laws of succession 1
leisure. 44, 47
Lewis, Dr. 76-77, 81n
Louis IX (king of France) 3
. . . . 4-5, 7, 66
love 22, 28, 32-33
Lovell, Sir Francis 24, 37n
Lyhert, Walter (bishop
   of Norwich) 31

M
Managier de Paris. 35-36
Mancini, Dominic . . . 28, 34, 71
Margaret of Anjou 2, 3, 5-6
   . . . 10n, 16, 17, 32, 37n, 62
   . . . . 63, 64-78, 81n
Margaret, duchess of
   Burgundy. . . . 17, 19n, 23-24
   . . . . 47, 79n
Margaret, duchess of
   York. 60
marriage 21-40
Mary I (Tudor) 78
Mary, duchess of
   Burgundy. 24
Maximilan I (Emperor). . . . 37n
Molynes, Lord 59
Mowbray, Anne 21
Mowbray, Catherine
   duchess of Norfolk 22
Mowbray, John, duke
   of Norfolk 22

N
Neville, Anne *see*
   Anne Neville
Neville, Ralph, first earl
   of Westmorland. 22
Neville, Richard (Earl of
   Warwick). 3-6, 22, 37n
   . . . . 67, 67n
nuns (religious). 13, 21

P
Paston, Agnes. 46
Paston, Elizabeth. . . . 14, 26-27

Paston, family of. 26
Paston, Margaret . . . 14, 16, 18n
  . . 30, 32, 42, 43, 44, 47, 59
Paston, Margery 14, 18n
   . . . . 30, 31, 32
peasant life. 21, 51-52
Philip, duke of Burgundy 3
   . . . . 5, 67
Plantagenet, Richard . . . .
   (Duke of York). . . . 1, 2, 22
Plumpton, Dorothy 14
pregnancy 53
Poynings, Richard 27
Powers, Elaine . . 13, 35, 46, 49

Q
Queen's College. 17

R
Ralph, Earl of
   Westmorland 61-62
Richard, Earl of
   Cambridge 10n, 37n
Richard, Lord Rivers
   (father of Elizabeth
   Woodville) 4, 69
Richard II 12n, 29
Richard III. 7, 8, 9, 23, 25
   . . . . . 32-34, 39n, 44, 47, 51
   . . . . . 60, 61, 71, 72, 73, 74
   77
   domestic policies. 9
Richard IV 21, 24, 61
   . . . . 72-73, 78-79, 79n

S
Scotland, army of 64-66
Scrope, Sir Stephen 26
Shore, Jane 36
Stafford, Henry (Duke
   of Buckingham) 9, 76
Stafford, Humphrey. 22
Stanley, Sir William 69
Stillington, Robert
   (Bishop of Bath &
   Wells) 9, 10
Swynford, Catherine . . 29, 37n

Swynford, Catherine *con't*—
   relation with court. 79

T
Thomas, Duke of
   Gloucester 12n
Thomas, Lord Stanley . . . 9, 72
Treaty of Picquigny 11n
   of Troyes. 38n
tuberculosis 11n
Tudor, Edmund 76
Tudor, Henry *see*
   Henry VII *and/or*
   Henry VIII
Tudor, Jasper . . 27, 38n, 68, 76
Tudor, Owen 30, 76
Twynko, Ankarette 7

V
virginity. 1, 36

W
Wales, role of, in conflict 7
War of the Roses 2, 59-78
Warbeck, Perkin . .24, 47, 72-79
Warwick's Rebellion. 3-7
Westminster cathedral .8, 24, 74
William, Lord Hastings 28
William, Lord Herbert 76

Woodville, family of. 4, 22
Woodville, Catherine
duchess of
Buckingham 12n, 27
Woodville, Elizabeth *see*
Elizabeth Woodville
Woodville, John 4
Woodville, Richard 4
women
   and war 59
   controlled by men 27
   equality with men 20n
   feared by men. 50
   in business 35
   in guilds. 50
   loyalty of. 59-78
   male attitudes toward. 35, 77
   mortality of 53
   singleness of 1, 35
   warriors. 59-78
   work of 14-15, 41-58
wool 50-51

ABOUT THE AUTHOR

Darlene Kay Tempelton was born in San Diego, California. She took her baccalaureat degree in history at the University of San Diego. She received the Master of Arts degree in Religion from the University of Dayton in Ohio.

Ms. Tempelton teaches at Catholic Central High School in Springfield, Ohio. Currently she is co-researching the life of women in medieval England; it is to appear later in this series.